THE SOUTH AFRICAN CULINARY TRADITION

The origin of South Africa's culinary arts during the 17th and 18th centuries, and 167 authentic recipes of this period

Renata Coetzee

Colour photographs by Volker Miros

C. Struik Publishers
Cape Town

C. STRUIK PUBLISHERS
OSWALD PIROW STREET, FORESHORE, CAPE TOWN

First edition 1977
Second impression 1979
Third impression 1981
Fourth impression 1984
Fifth impression 1988

Copyright © Renata Coetzee 1977

Designed by Shirley Friedman, Cape Town
Lithographic reproduction by UCA Repro (Pty) Ltd, Cape Town
Typeset by McManus Bros (Pty) Ltd, Cape Town
Printed and bound by Tien Wah Press (Pte) Ltd., Singapore

ISBN 0 86977 083 7

Half-title: Plump sweet raisins, complete with seeds and stalks and fermented with sugar, provide the leavening agent, or 'must', for aniseed-flavoured *mosbolletjies* and *tempies*. Flour for these traditional buns was stored in a yellowwood *meelkis* (shown here) and the long-handled peel was used to shovel them into the oven. Any leftover buns were stored in the big calabash.

Frontispiece: Even in the simplest country cottage the housewife would pride herself on her jam-making. The finished product was stored in earthenware jars kept tightly sealed with stretched and dried ox-bladders. Here, served in a rustic setting, is fresh-baked bread spread with rendered fat and grape (right) and sour fig (at left) preserves.

'For what we have to eat and drink,
We praise thy name O Lord!'

Translation of a traditional grace often sung at table

CONTENTS

ACKNOWLEDGEMENTS

A book of this kind can hardly be written without drawing on the experience and knowledge of people who, since childhood, have been acquainted with traditional South African cookery and the milieu in which it developed.

To the following special thanks are due for their assistance: Dr Anna de Villiers who spent her childhood on the farm Saxonburg in the Kuilsrivier district and is an authority on the culture and customs of the Afrikaner woman.

Mrs Crystal Campbell who grew up on the farm Groot Paardevlei, Somerset West, and who has an intimate knowledge of the edible wild plants which were eaten at the Cape in days gone by.

Prof. Mattie E. Jooste who was born on the farm Bellevue in the Tulbagh district and who is an authority on, as well as the pioneer in, the scientific study of South African cookery.

I am especially grateful to Volker Miros and his staff for the magnificent photographs; their combined skills and artistry are clearly evident in the colour pages that contribute so much to this book.

My sincere thanks are also due to the following people and institutions who singly and together assisted in this project with their knowledge, expertise, hard work and generosity: to Maretha Fourie and Magdaleen van Wyk who painstakingly prepared the dishes that appear in the photographs; to Marius le Roux and the staff of the Stellenbosch Museum; to Mr C. Cochrane, Miss L. Bibb and the staff of the Drostdy Museum, Swellendam; to Miss C. van Zyl and the staff of Koopmans de Wet House, Cape Town; to Mr and Mrs N. Myburgh, Meerlust, Stellenbosch; to the Cultural History Museum, Cape Town; to Mr G. Boonzaaier, Blaauwklippen, Stellenbosch; to Oude Meester-Stellenryk Wine Museum, Stellenbosch; and to Mrs J. Faure, Mrs B. Louw and Miss W. M. Currey; all of whom lent us authentic period pieces for the photographs and, wherever possible, permitted the photographs to be taken in genuine settings.

Finally, I would like to thank Oom Kosie Gericke for his help in checking the information contained in this book, and the numerous other people without whose help this book could not have become a reality.

Renata Coetzee
1977

FOREWORD

From time to time food connoisseurs are so inspired by old Cape cookery as it is still practised today, that they set out to discover the origins of traditional dishes. Renata Coetzee is such a person; she has devoted much of her time to tracing the sources and development of this culinary art and the results of her untiring research are recorded in this book.

The South African Culinary Tradition presents a clear picture of mealtime customs during an important part of our history, from 1652 to the end of the 18th century. The methods and discipline which Renata Coetzee acquired during her studies for an M.Sc. degree in Home Economics at the University of Stellenbosch, and later as dietician, enable her to approach with insight the interrelation of cultural background, eating habits and social life of the early Cape-Dutch community. The interest shown by C. Struik Publishers in producing a book on this subject provided an important additional incentive. Renata Coetzee presents old-time recipes in everyday language and the measures and quantities of the ingredients in current terms, while at the same time retaining their original character and distinctive charm. Her book is richly imbued with the romanticism of the culinary art of the 17th and 18th centuries in South Africa.

To every South African who is interested in this country's past, and also to the stranger who wishes to become better acquainted with historic Cape cuisine, this useful work offers enjoyable reading.

Mattie E. Jooste, M.Sc. (Home Economics), Ph.D., Emeritus Professor of Home Economics, University of Stellenbosch, 1976.

C.D. BONE ESPERANCE

C. Allard exc. cum Priv. ord. Holl. et Westfr.

CABO DE BÕA ESPERANÇA

*The 15th century saw a gradual change in the world map,
for Portuguese mariners, bent on discovering a new route to
the East, were reaching ever farther on their voyages of
discovery down Africa's unknown western seaboard.
Eventually, in 1486, they successfully rounded the
continent's southern tip and from then on the Cape featured
prominently on all their charts. At first, because of the
violent seas churned up by its strong prevailing winds, it
was known as* Cabo Tormentoso, *or the Cape of Storms,
but happily this name was short-lived; soon it came to be
called* Cabo de Bõa Esperança, *or the Cape of Good
Hope, for the dream of a sea-route from Europe to the East
had at last become a reality.*

*By the mid-17th century the Cape had won further renown
as 'the tavern of the seas': symbolically, Table Mountain
beckoned to all seafaring gourmets to pause a while and
enjoy the Cape table.*

3 Fresh meat, fruit and vegetables were provided by
Commander van Riebeeck's garrison to passing travellers.
Only six months after the first seeds were sown in the
Company's Garden visiting ship's officers were treated to a
meal consisting entirely of home-grown produce.

SOURCES OF ILLUSTRATIONS

Africana Museum, Johannesburg: 6, 10, 11, 23, 29, 31, 32, 37, 39, 52, 53, 67, 70, 77

Bogaert, A., *Historische Reizen Door d'Oostersche Deelen van Asia:* 5

Cape Archives, Cape Town: 3, 4, 9, 14, 15, 19, 21, 49, 58, 60, 65, 68, 76

Curtis's Botanical Magazine: 30, 36

De la Rochette (Private Collection, Cape Town): 20

De Verstandige Kock: 78

Forbes, W. A., *Antiek Bestek:* 45

Grosvenor House Museum, Stellenbosch: 71, 74

Het Eerste Nederlandsche Gedrikte Kookboek: 38

Hopkins, H. C., *Die Moeder van ons Almal:* 58

Iconographisch Bureau, The Hague: 24

Killie Campbell Collection, Durban: 59

Kolbe, P., *Naaukeurige en Uitvoerige beschrijving van de Kaap de Goede Hoop:* 13, 27, 40

Library of Parliament, Cape Town: 12, 22, 28, 35, 44, 46, 51, 54, 61, 66

Sijthoff, A. W., *De Volmaakte Hollandse Keuken Meid:* 50, 75

South African Illustrated News: 69

Walton, J., *Water-mills, Windmills and Horse-mills of South Africa:* 41

EQUIVALENT MEASURES

This collection of recipes has been compiled from many old handwritten sources, from cookery books published since 1890, from traditional family recipes acquired from interested parties, and from modern cookery books containing traditional recipes. From these many and varied sources I have selected those recipes that most closely depict the culinary practices of days gone by. The housewife of those days had to measure ingredients in terms of her kitchen equipment and her own experience. She had to decide for herself how large a tea-cup or a wine-glass was and what quantity was meant by a 'little' sugar or a 'heaped spoon'.
Therefore, to assist people in following old recipes, I have provided these rough guidelines:

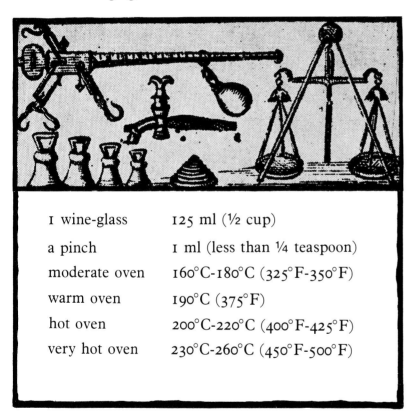

1 wine-glass	125 ml (½ cup)
a pinch	1 ml (less than ¼ teaspoon)
moderate oven	160°C-180°C (325°F-350°F)
warm oven	190°C (375°F)
hot oven	200°C-220°C (400°F-425°F)
very hot oven	230°C-260°C (450°F-500°F)

CHAPTER ONE
FOOD FOR
THE CAPE TABLE

'*Strandlopers*' was the very descriptive name given to the indigenous people of the Cape in the 17th century. Theirs was a care-free existence: they neither cultivated crops nor tended cattle and, since they depended entirely upon veld and ocean for their sustenance, there was no stable food supply available for the voyagers who called at Table Bay at that time.

It was the Vereenigde Oost-Indische Compagnie, a great Dutch maritime and trading company, popularly known as the VOC, that gave the first impetus to food production at the Cape. In 1652 its central governing body – the Lords Seventeen – despatched a party of its officials to the Cape under the direction of Commander Jan van Riebeeck with orders to establish a revictualling station for passing ships.

5

Within 14 days of their arrival these early settlers had laid out a vegetable garden and, a month later on 13 May 1652, Commander van Riebeeck wrote to the Lords Seventeen requesting them to send more sweet potatoes and pineapples, seeds of watermelon, pumpkin, gourd, cucumber and radish, as well as vines and fruit trees for cultivation. In particular he asked for young orange and lemon trees for the value of fruit, especially lemons, in treating scurvy among sailors was recognised even then.

Although no time had been lost in establishing the vegetable garden, the settlement had at first to resort to those edible wild plants locally available for its own use as well as for treating the scurvy patients. For the first meal at the Cape wild mustard leaves (*Cruciferae*) were gathered as well as four sacks of sorrel (also known as yellow-dock because of its yellow flowers). The stem and roots of this plant were chewed or used in cooking, both for

4 Jan van Riebeeck's arrival at the Cape, 1652. The local Hottentot people – or *Strandlopers* – were of little help in supplying food for they lived entirely on shellfish and *veldkos*.   5 A Saldanier kraal on the northern shores of Table Bay. Van Riebeeck found cattle-trading with these Hottentot herdsmen unreliable and soon felt driven to desperation by their dishonesty. At this time wild animals, such as elephant, still roamed freely at the Cape.

their sour, tangy taste – the result of a high oxalic acid content – and as a substitute for lemons and vinegar. In addition, sorrel contains vitamin C (ascorbic acid) and was therefore useful in the treatment of scurvy. Another plant that was found locally was wild asparagus and this was uprooted in the veld and transplanted in the Company's Gardens.

Unfortunately the new settlers did not fare well with all the fruit they found in the veld for, according to the Commander's records, a soldier died after eating wild almonds *(Brabeium stellatifolium)*. This was not surprising for these plants contain prussic acid, though it was subsequently discovered that if the almonds were soaked in water, they lost their lethal properties and could be eaten quite safely. The Hottentots traditionally ate these almonds too, roasting them first to remove the poison. Tragic though the soldier's death was, it did not blind the Commander's eyes to the beauty of the handsome wild almond trees; indeed, he gave orders that they should be planted to form a hedge on his farm and parts of it remain in the National Botanic Gardens at Kirstenbosch.

Herbs

In the old days herbs from the herb garden were used in most kitchens. The herbs were hung in small bags from the Spanish reed ceiling beams to dry. The dried herbs were rubbed between the hands to remove the small leaves from the twigs and crushed into finer pieces. Johanna van Riebeeck wrote that dried herb twigs should be soaked in lukewarm water before shredding.

Herbs used at the Cape included basil, also known as koningskruid *or* steentym, *which was used in bredies. Use was also made of* bonekruid *and* groenkruid, *as well as mint and peppermint. Bayleaves were used in meat, fish and soup dishes; marjoram in sausage; rosemary with meat; parsley in soup; peach leaves in puddings; lemon leaves with meat; lovage in salads; thyme,* sitroentiemie *and sage with meat; sweet chilli (red or green) in curry dishes and fennel mostly in salads.*

Spices

Virtually all spices were imported from the East. The dried spices were usually pounded in a mortar when ground spices were needed. The types most commonly used were aniseed; coriander; cumin; caraway seed, also called koeksaad; *mustard; cloves; nutmeg; pepper (white, black and cayenne); pimento; Jamaica pepper, also called* naelbol; *chilli; ginger (dried as well as green); cinnamon; cardamom, dill and mace.*

6 The wild almond – *Brabeium stellatifolium* – is a handsome shrub with star-shaped foliage, but its fruits proved lethal when a young Dutch soldier ate them. Remnants of the hedge planted by Van Riebeeck to deter marauding Hottentots may still be seen on the eastern slopes of Table Mountain. **7** Chutneys and sambals – a blend of local fruit and exotic spices – are a heritage bequeathed to South Africa by Malay slaves. Also of eastern origin are the two dark stoneware storage pots, or martavans, which were brought to the Cape in ships laden with rice.

6

7

Throughout the years the beautiful gardens that Van Riebeeck left to posterity have continued to be a source of pleasure to people living at the Cape and visitors alike. An early writer, François Valentyn, called here four times between the years 1685 and 1714 and on each occasion waxed eloquent over the gardens he found at the Cape. The Company Gardens, he declared, were unequalled in their beauty; they were comparable, he wrote, with the legendary Gardens of the Hesperides in which grew the celebrated golden apples, or with the Hanging Gardens of Babylon so lavishly praised by writers of antiquity. This tribute might be paid with as

9

much justification today, except that the vegetable beds have made way for other, more spectacular plants, for trees and for colourful shrubs.

But success was certainly not instantaneous and at first the gardens proved disappointing, for rigorous winter storms destroyed one vegetable crop after another. All the same, the Commander's refreshment station progressed to such an extent that on 13 October 1652 – a mere six months after his arrival – he was able to treat the officers aboard the barque *Goede Hoope* to a farewell dinner at which they were served produce and livestock grown and raised locally. He offered them chickens, peas, spinach, asparagus and crisp, firm heads of lettuce each weighing as much as 560 g. Also on the menu was chervil *(Acetosella cerefolium)*, a pot-herb with leaves resembling parsley and tasting a little like aniseed. This was usually chopped fine and used to flavour soup, sauces, salads or boiled green vegetables.

Van Riebeeck took a pride in market-gardening and, in the ten years that he spent at the Cape, cultivated an impressive variety of plants. Meticulous notes of all crops, vegetables and fruit were kept in his horticultural record book, the *Caapsche Hoveniers Almanack (Cape Nurseryman's Almanac)*, which, unfortunately, has not been preserved, though from his *Daghregister (Journal)* we know that he grew lettuce, endives, spinach, red cabbage, cauliflower and Savoy cabbage, turnips, radishes, yellow beet and beetroot, carrots and parsnips, chervil, horse-radish, pumpkins, gourds, cucumbers, artichokes, fennel, chillies, watermelons and *spanspek* (cantaloups). In the Company Gardens several varieties of beans and peas were also grown and these were sometimes called *katjang* from the Malay word for nuts and legumes. This term, like many other Malay expressions and influences, was brought to the Cape in the earliest days of the settlement for at that

8 For her butter-making, the Cape housewife used a *stampkarring* or dash churn with its wooden, often star-shaped plunger. Salt was added and the last traces of buttermilk worked off in a *botterbak* made from a single piece of *waboom (Protea arborea)*, and finally a wetted mould was used to shape the butter into a neat block. **9** Ludwigsburg Garden, off what is today Kloof Street, was renowned for the variety of plants, both edible and decorative, that Baron von Ludwig cultivated there.

time the Dutch controlled Indonesia and the Company had its headquarters at Batavia (present-day Djakarta) on the island of Java. Also appearing on Van Riebeeck's table was black salsify (*Scorzonera hispania,* family Compositae), a root vegetable with black skin and white flesh which was eaten either boiled or baked. Then there was fennel (*Foeniculum vulgarae*), a herbaceous plant the leaves of which were chopped fine and added to salads and sauces. Its bulbous roots could be either boiled, stewed or baked and served as a vegetable. Although many of these varieties of vegetables are no longer generally served at the Cape, the sound practice of having many different kinds available was established here from the earliest times of Dutch settlement.

Jan van Riebeeck also ordered fruit trees to be planted in the Company Gardens and, because of the wide variety that soon became available, the Cape was before long able to meet its own needs. The inventory taken at his farm *Bosheuwel* (now Bishopscourt) when he left for Batavia in 1662 testifies to the success he achieved during the first ten years of fruit-growing at the Cape. His estate boasted 1 162 citrus trees, ten banana, two olive, 24 chestnut, 19 plum and 70 fruit trees from Holland, among them 24 walnut, six quince, five apple and 11 cherry trees. Although they are not listed in the inventory, it is recorded that peaches, apricots, guavas, medlars and mulberries had been planted in addition elsewhere.

Nor were berries overlooked. In a letter dated 14 April 1652, Van Riebeeck made a request that red, white and black currants,

10

blackberries and dewberries should be sent to the Cape to see whether they would thrive. Currants (*Ribes,* family Saxifragaceae) grow wild in Asia and the white, red and black varieties are cultivated in western Europe. The white are sweetest, but the red are more common as table fruit and for making berry juice, fruit wine, purées and jellies. Dewberries (*Ribes grossularia,* family Saxifragaceae) are also grown in western Europe and are yellow, green, red, purple and white in colour. Yellow dewberries are the sweetest and have the thinnest skin; when half-ripe they have a high pectin content and are used to make jelly, jam and purée. However, Abraham van Riebeeck, son of the former commander, while on a voyage from Holland to Batavia in 1676, recorded that dewberries and currants did not thrive at the Cape but that wild blackberries (*Rubus fructicosus*) were already established.

If Jan van Riebeeck had problems with the cultivation of fruit and vegetables at the new refreshment post he had no grounds for complaint as far as grapes were concerned. Best known of all Cape fruit, they succeeded from the start and vines of well-established varieties were imported from Spain, France, Italy, the Netherlands, Brazil, St Helena, Batavia, Amboina, Japan and Madagascar. According to the historian Godée Molsbergen, Van Riebeeck himself was responsible for the development of the hanepoot grape which, with its distinctive flavour, won a special place for itself on the Cape table and was used extensively in old recipes.

It was Jan van Riebeeck's ambition that the Cape should press its own wine and on 2 February 1659 he was able to record joyfully

11

in his Journal that on that day wine was made for the first time. Not long after his departure for Batavia the wine from *Bosheuwel* was described as being 'extremely good and palatable' and a further interesting comment was made by his son Abraham who, 14 years later, wrote that 'the Cape wine has the colour of French wine, yet tastes a little of the fennel which is used to scour the vats'. It was important that the wine produced here should be of good quality for seamen and workmen received a ration which at first had to be imported from Spain or France. Sometimes this was supplemented with arrack, a spirit distilled from rice and imported from the East, and to provide a local substitute attention

10 *Grewia occidentalis* – one of the edible indigenous plants found at the Cape. 11 Once a familiar Cape sight – a barrel is carried through the streets.

23

was turned to the production of brandy. A certain Jan van Passel from the province of Antwerp was one of the first free burghers and when he began farming in 1657 he was given permission to distil brandy. At one stage hops were planted and beer brewed according to a recipe used in Cologne.

Wine, brandy and beer were served with meals, even at breakfast, for coffee and tea were still virtually unknown; in fact, these beverages were not even mentioned in Van Riebeeck's Journal. The first reference to the custom of tea-drinking is made in a letter written by Abraham van Riebeeck from the Cape in November 1676: in this he remarks that on one occasion he 'refreshed himself with a tea drink'.

In time the consumption of alcohol got somewhat out of hand and in 1669 the authorities were obliged to reduce the number of approved public houses from 20 to seven. The two taverns at the Cape Fort were allowed to serve only '*Mom*', a strong beer brewed in Brunswick, and French wine, while the other publicans sold brandy and arrack. In an effort to keep the free burghers from frequenting these places they were encouraged to increase their grain production instead, and the price of a muid of wheat and rye was raised.

The cultivation of grain at the Cape was slow to develop for time and again storms destroyed the crops. As a result almost every ship from the East had to bring with it supplies of rice and also of bread. This was better known as ship's biscuit for it had to be dehydrated to prevent it from turning mouldy. In addition to

12

24

wheat, Van Riebeeck sowed rye, barley, oats, buckwheat and maize (or Turkish wheat), but it was only after he had compelled the free burghers to plant cereal crops that grain production began to show any substantial improvement.

The Commander's repeated efforts at cultivating rice were doomed to failure and for this he had to face the censure of his superiors. As in the Netherlands and Batavia, rice was an important item in the diet: it was the staple food of slaves and prisoners and supplies had to be constantly shipped to the Cape. This was much to the dissatisfaction of the authorities who, in March 1657, were obliged to issue orders for even larger quantities to be imported and it was at this time that the custom of serving rice with certain Cape dishes became established – a tradition that continues to the present day. Potatoes, on the other hand, became known in Europe and at the Cape only towards the end of the 17th century.

13

One of Van Riebeeck's problems was the provision of sufficient fresh meat for the needs of passing ships as limited cargo space and the long voyage meant that to bring large numbers of livestock to the Cape for breeding purposes was out of the question. The Strandlopers were not cattle-owners and the Commander's only alternative was to barter for stock with the Saldanhers, or Saldaniers, who lived near the present-day Saldanha Bay. But these Hottentot people were certainly not over-anxious to part with their livestock and the animals they were prepared to barter were their very poorest. Predators and theft reduced the meagre herds at the settlement yet further and although Van Riebeeck had announced with pride on 9 January 1653 that there were at the Cape Fort 350 sheep and 130 head of cattle – including 25 milch cows – and that these animals were slaughtered for meat only on rare occasions, so great were the subsequent losses that on 20 October of the same year only 60 sheep, one ox, one milch cow and four calves remained. After two years of struggle, a start was made with the breeding of sheep and hares on Robben Island. Pigs were also imported in a further attempt to satisfy the ships' needs for fresh meat, but even this by no means solved the problem. The scarcity of meat meant that the Commander had to make use of all possible resources and consequently dassies, seagulls and penguins made their appearance on the table. The desire for meat was

Pickled fish

The best fish to use is Cape salmon (geelbek) and cob (kabeljou), but snoek or other firm-fleshed fish may also be used.

3 – 4 kg raw fish
30 g (2 tablespoons) salt
6 large onions, sliced and sautéd
2 lemon or bayleaves
2 chillies
60 g (half cup) curry powder
5 ml (1 teaspoon) turmeric
25 ml (2 tablespoons) sugar
12 peppercorns
1,25 – 2l (4-6 cups) good quality vinegar

Cut the fish into 25 mm slices, sprinkle with salt and leave to stand for a few hours. Then fry or steam the fish until cooked. Meanwhile make a sauce by cooking all the other ingredients together and while still hot, fill an earthenware casserole with layers of sauce and fish. When cold, cover securely and leave to stand for a day before serving.

12 Piquant, aromatic, exotic – in food and character the Cape Malay has had much to contribute to the spice of local life. **13** Milking a Hottentot cow. Commander van Riebeeck soon realised that the local cattle were of poor quality.

Game

Several authors mention game dishes of which little is known today. We read for example that porcupine meat was served to Augusta de Mist when she accompanied her father, Commissioner de Mist, on an official journey into the interior in 1803. The determined endurance of this nineteen-year-old girl won the admiration of all who met her.

The skin of the porcupine was considered a rare delicacy. This recipe was reproduced by Miss Allie Hewitt in her 1890 cookery book, Cape Cookery, Simple yet Distinctive. *The spines are plucked and the hair singed off. After the skin has been scraped clean, it is soaked for 24 hours in brine and then boiled in fresh water. It is then cut into strips, broiled over live coals and served with butter and lemon.*

A wide variety of game formed part of the diet in those days, as is apparent from Johanna Duminy's description of their heavily laden wagon which contained four bontebok, three porcupine, five live steenbuck, three live crows (possibly kept as pets), thirteen tortoises and a basket of crabs. On the way, she wrote, they encountered many rhebuck and ostriches. She also records that they sat down to a meal of soup, game and potatoes.

Pot-roasted leg or chine of venison

Lard the meat with long strips of speck and place in an earthenware or porcelain dish. Leave for three days in a marinade of:

750 ml (1 bottle) red wine
500 ml (2 cups) vinegar
4 bayleaves
12 peppercorns
8 cloves
2 onions, sliced

Turn meat twice a day. Then cook the meat until tender, using the Cape pot-roast method (p. 94). Strain the marinade, thicken with flour and baste the meat with it. Braise for about 15 minutes, until brown.

Stewed venison

The forequarter of a buck can be appetizingly prepared in the following way. Place the meat in a heavy-bottomed saucepan. Add a few cloves, allspice, salt and pepper according to taste, as well as two cups (500 ml) of red wine, two cups (500 ml) water, a few pieces of speck and lemon peel. Stew slowly until the meat is tender, then add a lump of butter and thicken the sauce with a little flour. Serve with stewed sweet potatoes (p. 34).

14

such among the settlers that Van Riebeeck sang the praises even of dassie: he wrote that these animals were the size of six-week-old sucking pigs and that theirs was the best meat he had ever tasted – even preferable to lamb! The discovery that penguin eggs were palatable was a happy one for ever since then they have been regarded as a special delicacy.

At that time big game was still plentiful but the settlers had yet to acquire skill as hunters and, besides, their fire-arms were so clumsy that this source of food – a delicacy in itself – seldom served to fill the cooking pots. In later years venison tastefully prepared was served almost every day and readily offered to visitors from abroad.

Because of the initial shortage of meat and other fresh food the

15

early settlers relied on the ever-abundant supply of fish, and on the day after Van Riebeeck's arrival men sent ashore to seek food for the exhausted sailors caught no fewer than 750 steenbras. There were many varieties of fish at the Cape and Van Riebeeck declared them to be even more delicious than the fish with which he was familiar in his homeland – and after which the Dutch settlers named those that they found at the Cape. Cape snoek which is used in so many traditional dishes was originally known as *zee-snoeck* to distinguish it from the Dutch fish of the same name which is however a fresh-water variety. Van Riebeeck also records that rock lobster were caught in the rich Cape waters so in this respect, at least, it did indeed seem that they had come to the promised land.

14 Big game was plentiful but cumbersome fire-arms made it difficult to shoot the animals. Sometimes the most ingenious traps were devised. **15** Cape waters abounded in fish and the local people were adept at catching them, even with their bare hands.

27

CHAPTER TWO

THE DEVELOPMENT OF CAPE COOKERY

Braised fish

1 kg snoek or other fish
2 onions, sliced
2 potatoes, shredded
1 chilli, chopped

Steam the fish until done, remove the bones and flake into fine pieces. Sauté the onions and add the chopped chilli and a pinch of pepper. Slowly braise the fish and potatoes in the onion mixture. Sprinkle with cayenne pepper and serve with rice.

Lobster paté

Remove the meat from cooked lobster tails. Mince thoroughly – or mix in blender – and add the roe, if any. For every 500 g of lobster, add:

5 ml (1 teaspoon) pounded mace
2 ml (half teaspoon) pepper
1 ml (quarter teaspoon) cayenne pepper
50 g (4 tablespoons) sheep's tail fat or butter
35 ml (3 tablespoons) stock

Mix well, add salt to taste and bake in a pie dish in a medium oven (180° C) until golden brown.
Serve cold.

Lobster kedgeree

Sauté a few onions and add pieces of cooked lobster. Sprinkle with a little salt and pepper and the juice of one lemon. Add chopped chilli and a knob of butter and cook, stirring gently until the lobster is lightly browned.
Serve very hot on boiled rice with a little chutney.

16 Delicious when freshly caught and grilled over the coals, harders are among the most tasty of Cape fish. Lemon, onion juice, bay leaves and coarse salt enhance their subtle flavour.

How were all these delicacies for the Commander's table prepared – the rock lobster which was so plentiful or the fresh vegetables of which he wrote with such enthusiasm?

Old Cape documents have very little to say about the preparation of food, yet there are many references to herbs and spices either grown locally or imported. From this we gather that food was generously flavoured according to the taste acquired by the Dutch in the 17th century after their introduction to the spices of the East. Van Riebeeck refers, among others, to mace, cinnamon, aromatic rosemary, laurel leaves, sage, aniseed, parsley, fennel, pepper, cloves, nutmeg, red and green chillies, leeks and onions. Oil and vinegar were imported in Chinese martaban jars, and salt was collected from the pans at Salt River. A genuine Cape innovation was the use of the rendered fat of fat-tailed sheep, and this, so Van Riebeeck claimed, added a special flavour to the food.

In his Journal Van Riebeeck seldom refers to his wife, Maria de la Queillerie: her name is mentioned only in connection with the birth of three of her children – two sons and a daughter – at the Cape. On another occasion we read that she was present when the first two oranges were picked in the garden of the fort and from this we can gather that she shared her husband's joy and enthusiasm in the important market-gardening project. But it is almost certain that she did not help in the preparation of its produce for the table; four ship's cooks were responsible for all cookery undertaken at the fort. Two prepared the food for the table which the Van Riebeeck family shared with other officials, while the other two attended to the needs of the ordinary workmen. A distinction was made between them, though: for instance, the first radishes and lettuces were served only at the Commander's table but later, when vegetables were in abundant supply, the *arbeidsvolk*, as Van Riebeeck referred to the workmen, were also able to enjoy the fruits of their labours.

After the granting of farms to the first free burghers in 1657 their women began to prepare meals for their own families. Annetjie Boom, the wife of the head gardener, Hendrik Boom, set about this task with such enthusiasm that, on Van Riebeeck's suggestion, she opened the first inn at the Cape so that travellers from passing ships might be provided with meals and accommodation. Here she had many opportunities to try out new recipes, for it was estimated that approximately 6 000 sailors called at Table Bay every year. This resourceful woman earned for herself the nickname of *Annetjie de Boerin* (Annetjie the farmer) among her customers and friends for she also started the local dairy industry. As early as 1656 she had been granted the lease of the Company's cows and had undertaken the delivery of milk and butter. Butter-

Rissoles in vine leaves

Although the Dutch frickedillen in krop-salaet *is no longer made in Holland the recipe has been preserved at the Cape and the dish still appears on the table today. Mrs Dijkman's recipe dating from 1890 is as follows:*
'Take meat, vine leaves, pepper, salt, nutmeg, cloves and thyme, a slice of white bread and one beaten egg. Mince the meat, crumble or mince bread into it, mix with salt and pepper to taste and add the spices and egg. Rub each vine leaf with fat or butter, wrap around rissole, tie up with cotton, and place in a greased pot or pan – a pot is better because it has a lid. Eat with leaves and all. Do not allow to cook too dry. It may also be baked in an oven. For gravy, take a large knob of butter, roll in fine flour and stir into the pot after you have dished up the rissoles.'

17 Flavoured with spices and fresh herbs, rissoles in vine leaves are served with gravy in a rough clay bowl. This traditional Dutch dish is still enjoyed in South Africa, perhaps because vine leaves are more readily available here.

milk was popular, too, and was served in bowls to workmen and sick mariners. As the Dutch at this time were among the best cheese-makers in Europe it is not surprising that this was among the earliest industries to be introduced to the Cape. Probably cottage cheese was the first type made here but after Van Riebeeck had obtained the necessary cheese-making equipment it would have been possible to make sweetmilk and cumin cheese – two well-liked varieties at the time.

Baking, as an industry, was officially established in 1659 when free bakers were granted permission to practise their trade. At first they were licensed to make only bread and pies but before long they were also given permission to bake a special delicacy known as cracknel.

In his Journal Van Riebeeck has nothing further to say concerning the culinary arts during the settlement's first decade and for several years afterwards while food production at the Cape was still inadequate, eating habits remained simple. Indeed, the laying of the foundation-stone of the Castle in 1666 was celebrated with humble fare: a bean feast – presumably the traditional Dutch dish of dried beans stewed with bacon and onions. Nevertheless, Commander Zacharias Wagenaar, Van Riebeeck's successor and host at the festivities, made certain that although the menu might not be particularly inspiring the occasion would be a merry one, for he ordered eight barrels of beer for his guests.

From 1665 onwards local produce was sold at fixed prices at a market, or *passar*. The price-list below gives an indication of what went into cooking pots at that time and reveals to what extent the people were dependent on wild birds, game and fish:

Eventually the free burghers learned to adapt their farming

1 pound	Beef or veal	2 stuivers
1 pound	Mutton	3 stuivers
1 pound	Pork	4 stuivers
1 pound	Hartebeest, Eland, or Wild Boar meat	2 stuivers
1 pound	Rhinoceros, Hippopotamus meat	1 stuiver
1 Steenbok		16 dubbeltjes
1 Hare		8 dubbeltjes
1 Porcupine		10 dubbeltjes
1 Dassie		5 dubbeltjes
1 Wild Goose		6 stuivers
1 Mountain Duck		5 stuivers
1 Common Duck		4 stuivers
1 Wild Peacock		12 stuivers
1 Bustard		5 stuivers
3 pounds	Fresh Fish	1 stuiver
3 pounds	Salt Fish	2 stuivers
1 pound	Dried Fish	1 stuiver
1 Melon		½ stuiver
25 Turnips and Carrots		2 stuivers
1 measure	Milk	4 stuivers
1 measure	Buttermilk	2 stuivers
1 pound	Fresh Butter	12 stuivers
1 pound	Cape Cheese	8 stuivers
1 Hen's, Goose or Duck Egg		1 stuiver
2 Penguin Eggs		1 stuiver
4 Gull's or Cormorant's Egg		1 stuiver
1 pound	Wheaten Bread	1 braspenning
1 pound	Whole and Half-Rye	1 stuiver
1 pound	White Bread	1½ stuiver

Comparative values of old currency and today's South African cent:
1 stuiver was approximately equivalent to 3 cents
1 dubbeltje was approximately equivalent to 6 cents
1 braspenning was approximately equivalent to 5 cents

Bobotie

1 kg minced meat
1 large onion
25 ml (2 tablespoons) butter or oil
1 thick slice bread
250 ml (1 cup) milk
12,5 ml (1 tablespoon) apricot jam
50 ml (4 tablespoons) lemon juice
75 g seedless raisins
10 dried apricots
30 ml (2 heaped tablespoons) curry powder
12 almonds, quartered
5 ml (1 teaspoon) salt
2 ml (half teaspoon) pepper
6 lemon or bayleaves
2 eggs

Sauté the onions in the butter or oil. Soak the bread in half of the milk. Mix all the ingredients except the eggs, the remainder of the milk and the lemon leaves. Spoon into a casserole and press in the lemon leaves. Beat the milk and eggs and pour over the meat. Bake for approximately 45 minutes in a medium oven (180° C). Serve with rice, chutney, desiccated coconut and chopped nuts.

Fish bobotie

Hake (stockfish) is suitable for this dish. Prepare in same way as meat bobotie but use cooked, flaked fish instead of meat.

18 Bobotie is possibly the most popular dish of Cape Malay origin. A baked egg and milk sauce, spiked with lemon or bay leaves, tops a pungent blend of flavours – curried mince, apricots, raisins, nuts and herbs.

Stewed sweet potato

Peel 0,5 kg sweet potatoes. Cut into thick slices and place in a saucepan, add a little water, four tablespoons (60 g) yellow sugar, two tablespoons (30 g) butter, one strip of dried naartje peel and salt. Stew until soft. Add a little sherry just before serving.

Stewed green beans

500 g green beans, cut
1 large potato, sliced
Piece of rib of mutton
1 large onion, shredded

Place the beans, potatoes, onion and meat in a saucepan with a small amount of boiling water and simmer until the meat is tender. Flavour with salt and pepper and serve.

Carrots and cabbage were also prepared in this way. Vegetables, particularly squash and cauliflower, were served with melted butter and grated nutmeg.

Sousboontjies

125 g (1 cup) sugar beans
50 ml (1 tablespoon) vinegar
25 ml (2 tablespoons) butter
25 ml (2 tablespoons) sugar
5 ml (1 teaspoon) salt
2 ml (half teaspoon) pepper

Wash the beans and soak overnight. Drain and parboil in fresh water until almost soft and add the other ingredients. Allow to simmer and stir well to ensure that there is plenty of sauce.

Curried beans

2 kg fresh green beans
1 kg onions, finely chopped
750 ml (3 cups) vinegar
320 g (1,5 cups) sugar
25 ml (2 tablespoons) curry powder
20 g (3 tablespoons) cornflour

Steam the beans in a little salt water, drain, add two cups (500 ml) vinegar and all the sugar and bring to the boil. Mix the curry powder and cornflour with one cup (250 ml) vinegar and add to the beans. Stir until the cornflour is cooked. While hot pour into sterilized jars and seal. Curried beans may be preserved for a long time in sealed jars.

Quince, cucumber or onion sambal

Peel and grate or chop the fruit or vegetables into small pieces. Add a little salt, sugar, vinegar and finely chopped chilli.

Sambal is a delicious complement to curry dishes.

methods to conditions in their new homeland; food production increased and they eventually began to prosper, particularly after the arrival of Simon van der Stel as governor in 1679. With his knowledge of viticulture the quality of Cape wines improved steadily so that even before the year 1700 travellers were extolling the virtues of those produced at Constantia.

So well did food production at the Cape progress that by the end of the 17th century Simon van der Stel was able to write to the Lords Seventeen that the colonists lacked nothing: their cellars were well stocked with liquor, they had sufficient wheat in their lofts and there was no shortage of meat or fish in their larders. In these favourable circumstances cooking could be freely practised and soon came to acquire a distinctive character. Adam Tas, well-known Stellenbosch wine and wheat farmer, writing in his diary early in the 18th century, referred to the use of wine as a marinade in which to steep fish. Even at that early date Cape wine and brandy played an important part in local cookery and came to be used in many traditional recipes.

Among the visitors who called at the Cape early in the 18th century was Johanna Maria, granddaughter of Jan van Riebeeck. As the wife of the Governor-General of Batavia she must have been accustomed to the best of fare yet she wrote to her parents '. . . as for the food, it is better than that of Batavia'. She also praised the variety of fruit and this was understandable for by then she was able to pick it herself from trees planted almost 50 years earlier by

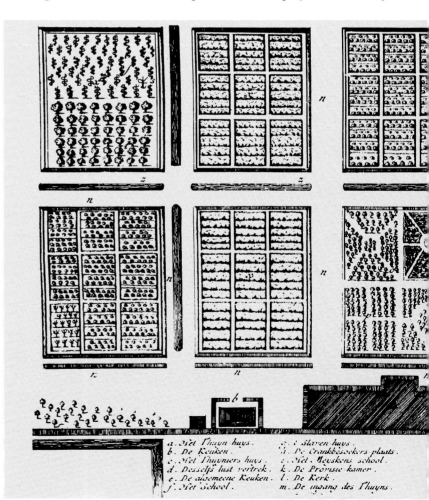

a. Het Thuyn huys.
b. De Keuken.
c. Het Thuyniers huys.
d. Desselfs lust vertrek.
e. De algemeene Keuken.
f. Het School.
g. 't Slaven huys.
h. De Crankbesoeckers plaats.
i. Het Meyskens school.
k. De Provisie kamer.
l. De Kerk.
m. De ingang des Thuyns.

her grandfather. She sent her parents fresh apples, pears and quinces as well as processed fruit, the description of which gives some indication of contemporary preserving methods used at the Cape. Quinces specially ordered for her by the former governor, Simon van der Stel, were preserved either by being salted and packed in a wickerwork container, or candied in what was described as a 'black dog' jar.

Several other world travellers of this period spoke with equal praise of the Cape table. François Valentyn was much impressed by the fruit and fish dishes that were prepared for him on several occasions, and Mary Ann Parker, wife of an English ship's captain who called at the Cape in 1791 while on a voyage round the world, was full of admiration for traditional Cape cooking. 'A meal in Cape Town,' she wrote, 'is distinguished by its substantial dishes and, what is most welcome to voyagers, plenty of vegetables which are as sweet as they can possibly be, for the situation of this climate is so happy that all European and most tropical fruits and vegetables grow as well as in their native soils.'

By the end of the 18th century Cape food had established a considerable reputation for itself among travellers who plied the Cape route between east and west. No doubt this was due to the ingenuity of hostesses who adapted their culinary skills to the climate and to the materials available. And among them was a certain woman affectionately known as 'Betje Bolletjie' in honour of the delicious koeksisters which she baked and sold.

Stewed dried fruit
Soak the fruit overnight and stew with a strip of naartje or orange peel. Serve with venison or leg of mutton.

Slaphakskeentjies (Cooked onion salad)
Small onions, peeled
2 eggs
25 ml (2 tablespoons) sugar
25 ml (2 tablespoons) vinegar or lemon juice
25 ml (2 tablespoons) water
Cook the onions in salt water until tender but not soft. To make a sauce, whisk the eggs with the sugar. Add the vinegar and water, stirring constantly and cooking slowly over boiling water until it thickens.

Green beans in sour sauce
Use tender young beans, clean, cut lengthwise and cook until soft. Make the sauce in the same way as for slaphakskeentjies *and pour it over beans. Serve cold.*

Guava salad
Peel and slice ripe oranges. Remove all the pips and pith. Peel and slice an equal quantity of ripe guavas. Arrange alternate layers of orange and guava slices in a glass dish and sprinkle a little sugar over each layer. Pour a wine-glass of sherry and half a wine-glass of orange liqueur or brandy over the fruit.

This charming old recipe makes a delicious dessert and as a salad it goes well with beef and venison dishes.

Water-cress salad
Wash the water-cress and break off the stalks. Put the leaves into a salad bowl. Make a dressing from the mashed yolk of one hard-boiled egg, a wine-glass of vinegar, half a wine-glass of sweet oil, a little prepared mustard and a pinch of salt.

This dressing may also be used for lettuce.

Tomato salad
Slice tomato and onions into salad bowl. Make a dressing from four tablespoons (50 ml) vinegar beaten with one egg and two tablespoons (25 ml) sweet oil, with a little pepper, salt and mustard. Traditionally this salad is garnished with slices of hard-boiled egg.

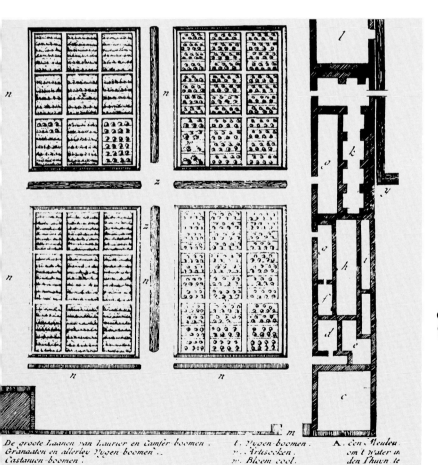

De groote Laanen van Laurier en Camfer boomen.
Granaaten en allerley Pygen boomen.
Castanien boomen.
Pompelmoes citroenen Limoen en Appel Sina boomen.
Bloemberg en Speelhuysie met Passie bloemen.
Wyngaarden.

t. Pygen boomen.
y. Artisocken.
z. Bloem cool.
x. Moescruyden.
v. Breede buyten grachten.
z. Waterleyding door den Thuyn.

A. een Meulen om t water in den Thuyn te malen.

19 A plan of the Company's Garden as it was in the early days of the settlement with the *Tuynhuys* overlooking it and a complex of buildings on the north side. Père Tachard, a visitor to the Cape in 1658, wrote: 'We were mightily surprised to find one of the loveliest and most curious gardens we ever saw . . .'

CHAPTER THREE
CAPE COOKERY IN THE 18TH CENTURY

South African culinary traditions should be seen against the background of Cape history and of the various groups of people who settled here. The romance and resources of the as yet unknown land at Africa's southernmost tip attracted many immigrants, and by the year 1700 the white population of the new colony had grown to approximately 2 000. Although from 1707 the governing body of the Vereenigde Oost-Indische Compagnie no longer paid the travelling expenses of prospective settlers, privately financed immigration and natural population increase led to a gradual growth so that by the end of the 18th century there were approximately 17 000 people living at the Cape.

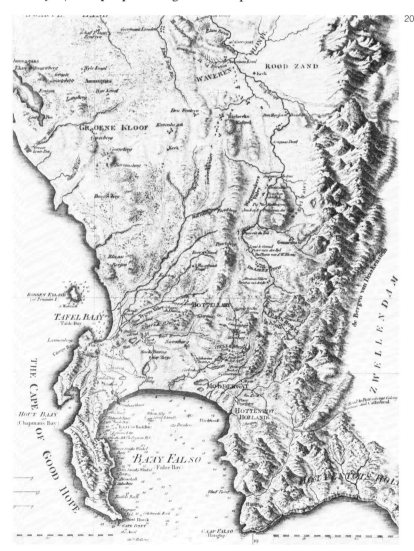

During the administration of the Vereenigde Oost-Indische Compagnie three different white communities evolved at the Cape. These were the original town-dwellers, the farming community settled on Boland farms, and the stock farmers or trek boers.

In Cape Town itself people lived on small farms at the foot of Table Mountain and Lions Head in the so-called Table Valley or *Caabse Vlek*. Judging from the number of citizens obliged to pay a fee for the services of a nightwatch, there were approximately 150 dwellings in old Cape Town at the end of the 17th century, but by 1784 these had increased to 1 200.

The first tentative expansion was southwards behind Table Mountain to Hout Bay, but boundaries continued to shift and, two years later, Governor Simon van der Stel inspired a new movement towards the north when, enchanted by the beauty of the Eerste River Valley, he chose the site for a new town – the first to be proclaimed in the interior. It was to be named after him – Stellenbosch – and to this day retains the grace and charm characteristic of every place which felt the impact of his personality.

The Cape of 1688 was to feel a new influence with the arrival of the French Huguenots. Not only did this mean an increase in the number of people living here but for the first time a settlement

grew up along the Berg River where they were granted farms. The plateau beyond the mountains was known as the Onderveld and, in contrast to it, the land stretching between the coastal plains and the Drakenstein range came to be called the Boland. On these beautiful farms, Cape cookery developed a distinctive character during the 18th century.

With a fine instinct for what was harmonious, the people both at the Cape and in the Boland adapted the architectural styles of their original homelands to local conditions and created their stately Cape-Dutch houses. As the climate was well-suited to the cultivation of grapes, fruit and grain, this produce, too, was to have an

20 The Cape Peninsula and its surroundings, 1782.
21 Groot Constantia. It was in this most elegant of Cape houses that Simon van der Stel entertained his guests to the best of Cape fare.

37

influence on the emergence of a distinctive building style. Houses and outbuildings were erected with thatched roofs and thick outside walls so that fruit and grain might be preserved within their cool interiors and the highly prized Boland wines might mature there to perfection. In time these estates became the homes of an established and prosperous community consisting of farmers whose backgrounds were Dutch and German as well as French.

At first the settlers in this area bought their slaughter animals locally from cattle farmers such as Henning Huising of Meerlust near Stellenbosch, but the demand steadily increased and in July 1700 Governor Adriaan van der Stel was obliged to move a number of colonists to the 'Land of the Waveren' which was also known as Roodezand and later as Tulbagh. They settled in this area as stock farmers but later trekked farther into the interior along the Breë River in search of suitable grazing for their animals, thus becoming the forerunners of the trek boers. Seven years later, however, Willem Adriaan van der Stel was relieved of his office and when colonists from the Cape were granted cattle posts beyond the Hottentots Holland Mountains and began to settle in the area, the original trek boers moved even further inland along the valley of the Riviersonderend. Some trekked northwards through the Swartland towards the Olifants River Valley and by 1745 the country had been opened up to such an extent that a new district and drostdy were established at Swellendam. When Governor van Plettenberg undertook his journey into the interior in 1778 he found trek boers living as much as 800 kilometres inland from Stellenbosch.

22

But isolation from the settled community of the Boland as well as constant encounters both with predatory animals and the indigenous peoples gave rise, during the 18th century, to a different way of life among the trek boers. They devoted themselves to stock farming rather than crop production and as a result new eating habits were developed to suit new circumstances. Fare such as *galopsop* and *skuinskoek* made its appearance while *gaat* – an infusion of the roots of the shepherd's tree – was drunk in place of coffee. *Galopsop,* a popular dish on the wagon-trail, was prepared by the rapid cooking of freshly-slaughtered meat for the midday meal, and *skuinskoek* was the name given to bread rolls cut into diagonal strips and deep-fried in hard fat. The soft fat was kept

38

aside for spreading on the rolls. These simple culinary practices developed to their fullest extent during the Great Trek in the 19th century but the character of the food remained that of its countries of origin and Dutch, French and German traditions were followed in the preparation. In time these were adapted to local conditions and, supplemented with Malay dishes, they developed, under a diversity of influences, into South Africa's distinctive and characteristic cuisine.

THE DUTCH ELEMENT

In the 16th century the Netherlands was well-known for its cultivation of vegetables which naturally led to their regular use in Cape cookery as well. The Dutch custom of serving vegetables – especially boiled cabbage, gem squash and potatoes – with a dab of butter and a sprinkling of grated nutmeg persisted, but unfortunately the weakness for lavish quantities of fat and butter was

23

Cinnamon pumpkin
For this side dish, peel and slice a boer pumpkin and cook until quite soft. Mash the pumpkin well and add sugar, salt, butter and ground cinnamon. Mix flour with a little water and add to pumpkin. Cook the mixture well, stirring to prevent burning. This dish should resemble thick porridge when cooked.

Baked pumpkin with cinnamon-sugar
Peel a boer pumpkin and cut into 50 × 100 mm segments. Notch and sprinkle with a mixture of sugar and ground cinnamon. Arrange in oven pans, add a little boiling water and salt, and bake in a medium oven (180° C) until lightly browned.

Pampoenmoes (breaded marrow or pumpkin)
Take a marrow or pumpkin, bread, butter, sticks of cinnamon, sugar and salt. Cut the marrow and bread into cubes. Arrange layers of marrow, bread cubes and pieces of butter in a saucepan and sprinkle each layer with sugar and pieces of stick cinnamon. Add a little boiling water and steam until done. Allow bottom layer to brown slightly, stir and serve.

22 The Drostdy, Swellendam. As the country opened up, traditional Cape hospitality extended into newly established towns and villages. **23** Smartly dressed and proud possessor of a rifle, a Hottentot hunter carries home his 'bag'.

39

adopted too. The writer of *De Volmaakte Hollandse Keukenmeid* – a popular Dutch cookery book of the period which, to judge from the copies in local museums, was much used at the Cape – warned readers to 'take care not to use too much butter . . . for butter makes the food too rich, too overpowering, too bilious, and is therefore unhealthy'.

In Holland meat and fish were always prepared with herbs and spices and were often marinated in wine, lemon or an infusion of rose petals known as rose-water. Ground or hashed meat dishes such as fricadels, and stews such as hotpot, frequently appeared on the Dutch table. Hotpot was a ragout prepared from meat and fat with the addition of potatoes, onions, cabbage or parsnips and originated in 1574 during the relief of Leyden after its siege by Spanish forces. Meals in the Netherlands also included intriguing roast dishes such as chicken stuffed with oysters or sucking pig stuffed with liver, prunes, currants and spices. These recipes were also used in the preparation of Cape meat and fish dishes which were deliciously flavoured by the addition of whatever herbs and spices were available. There were, however, many Dutch recipes which remained quite unchanged at the Cape and fricadels are still prepared here in the time-honoured manner though they are quite unknown in the Netherlands today.

Pies were extremely popular in 17th century Holland and fruit tarts made from apples and pears were a favourite dish both in the Netherlands and later at the Cape. Meat pies baked with both an upper and a lower crust were sold by the first free bakers while traditional Cape pies, such as those made from venison, chicken and saddle of lamb were to make their appearance locally in due course and occupy a prominent place on the menu.

In Holland, as at the Cape, pancakes and waffles were made in special long-handled irons over the open flames of the hearth fire. Pancakes were regarded as a particularly delicious dessert and, like waffles, were served with honey and cream. Another delicacy – *oblietjies* – consisted of a pastry of French origin in the form of thin, crisp wafers with ingredients similar in taste and flavour to old-fashioned *soetkoekies*. *Oblietjies*, too, were served with honey and cream and were cooked in long-handled *oblietjie* irons made specially for the purpose but in appearance very much like waffle

---

Oblietjies (rolled wafers)

2 eggs
450 g brown sugar
10 ml (2 teaspoons) ground cinnamon
10 ml (2 teaspoons) pounded naartje peel
120 ml (half cup) wine
250 g butter
450 g cake flour

Beat the eggs and sugar and allow to stand. Add the spices, wine and melted butter and fold in the flour. Form into balls the size of walnuts and place in the middle of the heated wafer iron. Close securely but without forcing. Bake for half a minute on each side until lightly browned and lift out with a spatula.

Roll up immediately into a trumpet shape or a roll open at both ends.

---

24 This painting is believed to be of Simon van der Stel on his return from the hunt with his hounds and his horse. Game has long been regarded as a delicacy on South African tables. **25** Of French origin and pre-dating the emigration of the Huguenots are wafer-thin oblietjies, delicately flavoured with naartje peel, spice and brandy. After baking the walnut-sized ball of dough in a beautifully impressed iron pan – which was probably imported from Sweden – the cook would skilfully roll the oblietjie into a crisp cone. Tradition has it that the name 'oblietjie' was derived from the words 'Hoc oblatum est', spoken by the priest as he raised the fragile unleavened bread of the Host during the Latin Mass.

24

25

irons. Clearly, therefore, 17th century Dutch culinary customs left their imprint on Cape cookery.

THE GERMAN CONTRIBUTION

Ever since the first ships revictualled at the Cape, German sailors had called at the refreshment post or even made it their home. Later their number was strengthened by the arrival of artisans, teachers and travellers, but as most of these arrived as bachelors and married local girls, German culinary traditions did not exert a profound influence at the Cape. Nevertheless, the German contribution is clearly discernible in the wide variety of boerewors recipes which evolved and have been maintained until the present.

A FRENCH FLAIR

The French Huguenots left their homeland long before famous and sophisticated chefs such as Carême, Montagne, Escoffier and Carrier created their recipes or the well-known restaurants of the 18th century opened their doors. For this reason the French influence on Cape cookery is a homely one for it had its origins in the French domestic kitchen of the 17th century.

Even though it lacked the lavish embellishments, the frills and flourishes of a Carême, French cooking undoubtedly enlivened the established Cape cuisine. The practice of draining all surplus fat from food, of flavouring it delicately with herbs and using spices sparingly, imparted a subtler character to the stolid Dutch food. Dishes such as hotpot from Holland, made way for lighter and less rich fricassees of the kind prepared in the south of France. Later the traditional Cape stew, under the Malay influence, changed its name to 'bredie', which, according to Dr Lichtenstein, a young German medical practitioner who lived at the Cape from 1805 to 1806 and was physician to General Janssens, meant 'spinach' in the old slave language. Another important innovation was that of serving dishes in sequence instead of simultaneously. Before this the Dutch – and therefore the Cape – custom was to place all the food on the table at once with the largest platter on which the meat joint was served in the centre. The other dishes which contained additional meat, poultry, fish and vegetables were so arranged that they formed a balanced whole – poultry opposite poultry and vegetables opposite vegetables. However, under French influence, soup was served before the main course and dessert, particularly fresh fruit, afterwards. This change in the presentation of food was the first suggestion of what have today become menu courses.

The sauces for which French chefs are so justly renowned were originally thickened with breadcrumbs instead of a mixture of butter and flour (roux). At the Cape sorrel was added to make a piquant sour sauce which was served with fish or meat dishes.

Our French forebears also handed on their methods of preparing those parts of the carcase known as offal. On his journeys into the interior Dr Lichtenstein became familiar with a characteristic South African dish which he called 'pens en pootjies', or tripe and trotters, and was most impressed with the hygienic methods observed by the housewife in its preparation. The meat was sometimes cooked inside a sheep's stomach which thus served a

Naartje peel
In the old days there was always a jar of dried naartje peel on the kitchen shelf. This was used to flavour pastries, glazed sweet potatoes and other dishes. A small piece was also kept in the tea caddy to impart a slight citrus flavour to a steaming cup of tea.

Remove the naartje peel in strips and dry in the sun or in the oven. When it is dry and hard, store in an airtight jar. Orange peel may be preserved in the same way.

Peach leaves
Infuse peach leaves in warm milk or water to add an almond flavour to food. Use in custard or pudding to add a delicate almond flavour.

Fig leaves
Simmer young fig leaves in water until the water is green and has a distinctive fig flavour. Strain and make a syrup by adding to every cup (250 ml) of water, one cup (200 g) of sugar, one tablespoon (12,5 ml) lemon juice and a pinch of salt. Use the syrup to prepare liqueurs, or serve with bread and butter.

26 Coarse meal used in bread-making was stone-ground in water-mills such as this one. The sacks were made from sheep skins removed in one piece from the animal's carcase and when a bag was accidentally torn it was repaired with the utmost skill.

Pickles and chutney

Do not allow any metal to come into contact with chutney or pickles during cooking or storing. Use a wooden spoon and if jars have metal tops, cover with wax paper or with paraffin wax.

Pickled cauliflower

1 cauliflower
25 ml (2 tablespoons) turmeric
25 ml (2 tablespoons) pepper
25 ml (2 tablespoons) sugar
Pinch of salt
25 ml (2 tablespoons) ground ginger
5 ml (2 tablespoons) mustard
Enough vinegar to cover the cauliflower

Break cauliflower into small pieces and sprinkle with salt. Pack into sterilized jars. Mix the other ingredients and bring to boil. Pour the boiling mixture over the cauliflower and seal. Leave the pickles to mature in a cool spot for one to two months.

Pickled green tomatoes

3 kg green tomatoes
20 ml (1,5 tablespoons) mustard
100 ml (8 tablespoons) golden syrup
1 kg onions, sliced
15 g (2 tablespoons) curry powder
1,5 ℓ vinegar

Cut the tomatoes into thin slices and allow to stand overnight in brine. Wash, place in a saucepan and add the other ingredients. Simmer for half an hour. Spoon into sterilized jars and seal.

useful purpose at a time when cooking utensils were both scarce and primitive. A kind of sausage called *andouille* was made in this way as well and consisted of meat cut into pieces, spiced and sewn into the stomach of a sheep, ox or pig, and then cooked until tender before being smoked in the chimney. Another delicacy was made from sheep's brains tied up inside the omasum or leaf-stomach and cooked with offal.

Skilled farmers in their own country, the Huguenots made a major contribution to the improvement of viticulture and fruit production at the Cape. Under their influence apricots of a better

quality were cultivated and the drying of raisins was developed into a fine art. In this way they bequeathed an unrivalled legacy to Cape cookery in the form of *boerejongens* and *boeremeisies* (literally, farmers' boys and farmers' girls) which were raisins and apricots preserved in brandy, while from watermelon and other fruit they made delicious French confections or *confitures* which today are known at the Cape as 'konfyt'.

Undoubtedly the French settlers imparted a Gallic flair to local culinary customs but their influence was never a dominating one. At no time did they comprise more than one-sixth of the white population and because they lived scattered among the established Dutch colonists they very soon became assimilated.

AN EASTERN AROMA

Probably the most far-reaching influence on the cooking customs of the Cape was the result of the importation of Malay slaves from

27 Ploughing at the Cape. The Hottentots took enthusiastically to pipe-smoking introduced by the settlers and tobacco soon became a vital item of barter.   **28** A Malay fish-hawker, wearing the traditional conical straw hat or *toering*. It was these people who transformed commonplace local fish into dishes to delight the most fastidious of gourmets.

whom South Africans have inherited a wealth of Eastern dishes. Referred to by one writer as 'kings of all slaves', they began to reach the Cape towards the end of the 17th century. The men were skilled carpenters, tailors, musicians, coachmen and fishermen, while the women were expert cooks who introduced not only exotic oriental dishes to Cape tables but brought with them the precious spices of the East. These included aniseed, bahia (star fennel), barishap (fennel), turmeric, cardamom, ginger both green and dried, gira (cumin seed), coriander, garlic, various mixtures of curry, mussala (a mixture of turmeric, gira and red

28

peppers), mustard seed, red pepper, saffron, saltpetre, sari leaves (an aromatic grass) and tamarind. Before long these spices were skilfully adapted to local circumstances and cardamom pods, green ginger and saffron made way in Cape curry dishes for such locally available flavouring agents as orange leaves, chutney and dried apricots.

The Cape Malays are past masters at combining a variety of spices in one dish or at serving 'hot' dishes with cool 'sambal' or, alternatively, hot chutney or pickles to add piquancy to bland foods. Basically, sambal consists of finely chopped vegetables or fruit steeped in salt and vinegar, with chillies, onions or other appetite-stimulating ingredients added according to taste. Possibly the best known varieties to become part of Cape cuisine were those sambals made from cucumber, quinces or onions, though the less widely known snoek sambal also originated here.

Cape Malay *atjar* or pickles consists, both locally and in the East, of vegetables and fruit, either whole or sliced, packed into a

Cape chutney

250 g dried apricots, cut into thin strips
500 g seedless raisins
500 g brown sugar
30 g (2 tablespoons) salt
3 ℓ vinegar
4 large onions, minced
60 g (4 tablespoons) ground ginger
30 g (2 tablespoons) pounded and sifted coriander
25 ml (2 tablespoons) pounded mustard seed
A handful of pounded red chillies

Soak the raisins and apricots overnight in vinegar. Add the other ingredients and boil very slowly, stirring all the time with a wooden spoon. Cook until the mixture is thick and drips slowly off the spoon. Spoon into sterilized jars and seal at once.

Quince or apple chutney

1,5 kg quinces or apples
250 g seedless raisins
1,5 ℓ vinegar
200 g (1 cup) sugar
30 g (2 tablespoons) salt
1 chilli, chopped
Half clove of garlic, chopped
12,5 ml (1 tablespoon) ground ginger

Peel and core fruit. Chop fruit into small pieces and place with all the other ingredients in a large saucepan. Simmer gently, stirring constantly. When the chutney is thick, spoon into sterilized jars and seal while still hot.

Clingstone peach chutney

1,5 kg clingstone peaches
12,5 ml (1 tablespoon) coriander
7 ml (half tablespoon) whole pimentos
750 ml vinegar
2 large onions, chopped
2 green chillies, chopped
50 g (quarter cup) sugar
7 ml (half tablespoon) cornflour
5 ml (1 teaspoon) salt
5 ml (1 teaspoon) turmeric
12,5 ml (1 tablespoon) curry powder

Peel and shred the peaches. Tie coriander and whole pimentos in a muslin bag and boil for a few minutes in vinegar. Make a paste from the sugar, salt, cornflour, turmeric, curry powder and a little of the vinegar. Combine all the ingredients and simmer until chutney is thick, remove the spice bag, spoon into jars and seal.

Date chutney

500 g seedless dates
2 cloves of garlic, chopped
1 small onion, chopped
Pinch of salt
A handful of chillies, chopped
500 ml (2 cups) vinegar

Mix all ingredients in a saucepan and simmer, stirring all the time, until thick. Spoon into jars and seal.

jar and covered with a mixture of fish oil, turmeric, chillies, curry and garlic. The Cape recipe is not quite as potent as the oriental and three different kinds may be distinguished: sour, curry and mustard. *Atjars* that have stood the test of time are made from cauliflower, mixed vegetables, clingstone peaches, oranges, lemons or green tomatoes. Green mango, green coconut and green almond *atjar* were also made in days gone by and are still occasionally prepared as a special delicacy.

Chutney is made by cooking fruit or vegetables with flavourings such as chillies, vinegar, garlic, ginger and other spices until they form a pulp which may be thin enough to allow it to be poured, or quite thick. Traditional Cape chutney consists of apricots; it is thinner than the other varieties and has a sweet-sour taste. Originally Malay chutney was extremely strong, but its potency was gradually reduced after it reached the Cape so that the spices were less overwhelming yet the characteristic fruit flavour was retained. These stimulating sauces continue to be popular in South Africa, especially when served with curry.

Several references to curries in old documents indicate that they began to appear fairly generally on Cape tables shortly after the arrival of the first Malays. As early as 1740 Otto Mentzel, a German teacher who lived here for several years, mentioned 'kerrie-kerrie' dishes and, in 1797, Johanna Duminy who lived with her French husband François Renier in the Riviersonderend valley, wrote in her diary: 'When evening fell I had the candles lit, the children were given their supper and put to bed. At 9 o'clock we are going to have a delicious curry.' After a time these dishes were adapted to the taste of people living at the Cape so that the chillies and green ginger which were so important to the Oriental virtually disappeared from local versions.

Meat curries of Malay origin also became very popular and bobotie, sosaties, bredie and other foods of this kind are still among the most sought after and flavoursome of the old Cape dishes. Pinang curry (presumably derived from the Javanese word *pin'dang*) was also a great favourite and consisted of meat flavoured with tamarind seeds and fresh orange leaves. Leipoldt, the Afrikaans poet and gourmet, went into raptures over this dish and wrote: 'Do not suppose that pinang meat is just an ordinary curry . . . There is reason to assume that the ambrosia of which the ancient poets spoke so often was a kind of ginger chilli – pinang curry.' There was also denning curry – *dendeng* in Javanese – which was flavoured with tamarind seed and mace leaves, and the much-fancied sabanang curry.

Born fishermen, lively and colourful by nature, the Malays have had much to contribute to the romance and individuality of the Cape. It was they who transformed such commonplace fish as galjoen, Cape salmon, maasbanker, mackerel, hottentot, shad, stumpnose, steenbras, stockfish and mullet into delectable dishes, while snoek – a member of the barracuda family and choicest of Cape fish – became so much their own that they called it 'our food'. It was made into kedgeree; it was salted, braised, smoked or pounded according to Cape Malay recipes; it could be grilled, roasted or baked over coals and, in the early days, was often served with *moskonfyt* (grape syrup). Pickled fish or fish grilled over coals were and remain part of the Cape way of life, just as *bokkoms* (kippered Cape herring) were an integral item in the diet of people living too far inland to obtain regular fresh supplies. The word 'bokkom' is derived from the Dutch *bokking*, meaning herring or bloater, and is applied to salted, dried herrings and maasbankers as well as to other varieties of small fish.

Another speciality of the Cape Malay fishermen was fish soup. To make this they cooked the fish-head and bones to obtain a glutinous fish-flavoured stock and then, having seasoned it, thickened it with the minced flesh and rice. In the days when the spiny lobster (*Jasus lalandi*) was still abundant along Cape shores, soup made from it was very popular. Usually only the tail of this variety is eaten, for the claws are not as well developed as those of species found in other parts of the world, but the resourceful Malays made a delectable curry from this part of the body while the flesh itself was used for all manner of intriguing dishes such as rock lobster fricadels (rissoles) and kedgeree.

Curried lobster legs

Legs of several lobsters
250 ml (1 cup) stock
12,5 ml (1 tablespoon) curry powder
1 large onion, sliced and sautéd in fat or oil
A dash of tamarind or juice of 1 lemon
A pinch of salt and pepper
A few lemon leaves

Boil the lobster legs for a few minutes and split open. Combine all the other ingredients to make a sauce. Simmer the lobster in the sauce for half an hour. Serve on rice sprinkled with finely chopped parsley, and a pat of butter. Serve with a sambal.

Fish soup

2 large lobsters or the head and bones of any large fish
1 large shredded onion and/or chopped shallots
Fat or oil in which to brown the onions
25 ml (2 tablespoons) curry powder
12,5 ml (1 tablespoon) lemon juice
7 ml (half tablespoon) brown sugar
500 ml (2 cups) cooked potatoes
A few carrots and tomatoes
A few bay or lemon leaves
(A wine-glassful of sweet wine may be substituted for the curry powder and lemon.)

Place fish in a saucepan, cover in salt water and boil slowly for an hour. Strain and reserve the stock. Sauté the onions in fat or oil. Make a paste from curry powder, sugar, a little salt and lemon juice. Combine all the ingredients and simmer until well-cooked.

Ladle into soup plates and garnish with a few slices of hard-boiled egg. This soup may also be served over rice and garnished with lemon slices. To make a delicious cold soup, omit the curry and add sweet wine and a pinch of grated orange peel. Fish soup is a favourite of the Cape Malays.

At that time sea-ears or abalone – known here as *perlemoen* – as well as periwinkles and limpets were still common in Cape waters and the Malay folk used these too in their curries or, by way of a change, prepared them without the strong seasoning which disguised their delicate flavour.

So much part of the Cape table did Malay dishes become that bobotie with yellow rice and raisins was chosen as the representative South African dish in an international recipe book published in 1951 by the United Nations Organisation.

EDIBLE WILD PLANTS (VELDKOS)
AND THEIR INFLUENCE

It was only towards the mid-18th century that the trek boers first came into contact with the black people living far in the interior.

29 Red and white hottentot and yellowtail (at bottom). The day after Jan van Riebeeck's arrival his men enjoyed their first meal of the seafood for which the Cape is still justly famous.

They found that these folk kept livestock and cultivated certain types of crops such as those known as 'kaffircorn' *(Sorghum caffrorum)* and 'kaffirwatermelon' *(Citrullus lanatus)* which were subsequently grown by the white colonists as well. The black people's diet was supplemented with insects such as locusts, ants and bees – a practice never adopted at the Cape.

Lady Anne Barnard, wife of the Colonial Secretary at the Cape during the first British Occupation at the end of the 18th century, made some laconic observations on the eating habits of the Africans at that time. She noticed that the chiefs from the interior who visited the Castle ate only beef and mutton; they refused the pies, fish or chicken, and were completely unfamiliar with fish and even with fishing tackle. 'The fish, therefore, in their rivers,' she wrote with characteristic humour, 'live unmolested by creation's Lords.' Lady Anne also commented that the Hottentots ate their food without any flavouring whatsoever; not even salt was added to it.

CAPE EDIBLE WILD PLANTS (VELDKOS)

Both the Strandlopers and Bushmen made their contribution to the early Cape table in the form of veldkos – wild plants which, for the most part, retained their original names. Veldkos was the staple food of these peoples but, although it was of importance in combating scurvy among sailors, it never played a significant part in the diet of the Cape's white colonists. These plants are far less plentiful at the Cape than in other parts of the world, for example

30

30 Early spring brings *waterblommetjies (Aponogeton distachyos)* to Cape dams and vleis. The white flowers of this plant are prized for the delicious bredie they make when braised with mutton, wine and a dash of sorrel juice.
31 Rich in vitamin C, wild sorrel's tangy juice provided a substitute for vinegar while its leaves, which contain oxalic acid, were used for cleaning brass.

South America where tomatoes, maize and tropical fruits were discovered, but those that grow deeper in the South African interior are often of considerable nutritional value. For instance, the 'camaru' of the Karoo and Namaqualand (*Fockea* spp) – sometimes also known as *kambro* or *kameroep* – is a bulb measuring up to 50 centimetres and weighing ten kilograms which provides a substantial quantity of jam or stew. The fruit of the mangetti (*Ricinodendron rautanenii*), which is found in north-west Botswana and in South West Africa is extremely nutritious and to this day is a staple food of the !Kung Bushmen.

Undoubtedly the best known and most highly prized Cape veldkos is a bredie made from *waterblommetjies*, or *wateruintjies* (*Aponogeton distachyos*), a plant which is generally found in Boland dams and vleis but which occurs nowhere else in the world. This gourmet's delight is prepared by gently stewing the cleaned flower-buds and soft stems in braised fat mutton with a handful of crushed sorrel leaves added to give a touch of sourness. The best months to enjoy this dish are July and August when the flower-buds are at their plumpest.

Other veldkos bredies that were known on early Cape tables were those made from the flowers of *'vetkousies'* (*Carpanthea pomeridiana*), a variety of succulent, and from the veld cabbage (*Anthericum* spp) which has short pedicles below the flower-buds.

Bulbs of the *bloublommetjie-uintjie* (*Moraea fugax*) were much sought after as a vegetable. After being peeled, the bulb was sautéed in butter and had a very pleasant, chestnut-like flavour.

31

Bredies

This is the old Cape name for a dish of stewed fat mutton and vegetables. In the Malay language bredie meant spinach, but virtually any vegetable may be used. Brown and stew diced meat, onion and chilli – and potatoes if wanted. Half or three quarters of an hour before serving, add the vegetables and salt and sufficient liquid to make gravy.

Tomato bredie

1 kg mutton
1 onion, chopped
2 chillies, chopped
12 tomatoes, skinned and chopped
25 ml (2 tablespoons) sugar
Salt and pepper

Cut 1 kg mutton into pieces. Sauté the onion and chillies in a saucepan. Add the meat, cover and simmer, adding small quantities of water until almost done – about two and a half hours. Add tomatoes, sugar and a little salt and pepper, thicken with flour and simmer for a few minutes. Serve with boiled rice.

Green bean bredie

Prepare in the same way as tomato bredie with sliced green beans instead of tomatoes and no sugar.

Cabbage and cauliflower bredie

Break the cauliflower into pieces or shred the cabbage. Prepare in the same way as tomato bredie. Add grated nutmeg before serving.

Quince bredie

Prepare in the same way as tomato bredie but use cooked quinces as the vegetable.

Waterblommetjie bredie

Pick the flowerbuds or open flowers. Remove the stalks unless they are young and tender. Wash the flowers well and leave them to soak in salt water for a few hours. Use the following ingredients to prepare two large bunches of waterblommetjies:

1 to 1,5 kg rib of mutton or leg of mutton
2 medium-sized onions, sliced
1 spray of sorrel, finely chopped
250 ml (1 cup) water
250 ml (1 cup) white wine
Salt and pepper

Place the chopped rib or sliced boned leg of mutton in a heavy-bottomed saucepan and sprinkle with salt and pepper. Braise in a little fat or oil until light brown. Add the onions and continue to brown. Add the rest of the ingredients and stew slowly until the meat is tender. Stir as little as possible and add water if necessary. A few small potatoes may also be added. Serve the bredie with boiled rice.

Brandied figs

Figs not yet fully ripe
Castor sugar
Brandy

Peel the figs without removing the stalks. Pack into wide-necked jars, layering sugar and figs in the proportion 1 to 4, i.e. 125 g sugar to 500 g figs. Fill the jars with brandy and replace screw-tops without tightening. Place a piece of wood or folded cloth in the bottom of a saucepan and stand the jars up to their necks in water in the saucepan. Heat to boiling-point, remove at once and seal.

Brandied peaches

Yellow clingstone peaches
Brandy
Heavy syrup consisting of equal quantities of water and sugar boiled together.

Take firm, unblemished peaches. Plunge into boiling water for a minute and then peel. Boil in syrup until fruit is tender but still firm. Drain and pack into sterilized jars. Fill the jars with a mixture of brandy and syrup, using twice as much brandy as syrup. Seal the jars.

32 *Taaibos (Rhus lucida).* Its green berries were eaten by children as a special treat. **33** An oriental porcelain bowl and elegant Cape silver dishes set off brandied figs and grapes to perfection. The master of the household would enjoy these after-dinner delicacies between puffs of tobacco lit from coals glowing in the pierced copper *tessie*.

There are two species of wild fig, both of which grow as creepers on sand dunes and produce edible fruit. One of these is the sour fig (*Carpobrotus acinaciformis*), a succulent with bright green leaves and flowers varying in colour from yellow to mauve. It bears a gelatinous fruit from which jam is made, while the Hottentot fig (*Carpobrotus edulis*) – also a succulent but with long, upright, triangular leaves and large yellow flowers – is so sweet that it may be eaten fresh. A traveller who visited the Cape in 1815 recorded that konfyt was made from the Hottentot fig and served as conserve at afternoon tea.

When a crisp, fresh salad was required various kinds of wild lettuce were gathered in the veld as well as the water-cress (*Nasturtium officinale*) that grew along the water-furrows. From the rivers a variety of bulrush called 'palmiet' (*Prionium serrata*) was collected for its soft young shoots and these, too, were prepared as a salad, as were the young, sour leaves of the *vetkousie*. The juicy sprouts of wild asparagus (*Asparagus rubicundus*) – also known as cat-briar and grown by Van Riebeeck in his garden – resemble very closely the cultivated variety today, both in taste and in appearance, and these were served fresh with a tart sauce.

Tameletjies (stick-jaw)
400 g (2 cups) sugar
250 ml (1 cup) water
150 g (150 ml) pine kernels or almonds

Bring the sugar and water slowly to the boil, stirring until sugar is dissolved. Allow to boil briskly until it froths and add pine kernels or almonds or grated orange or naartje peel or orange blossoms. Spoon into square containers made of folded paper. Allow to cool completely before eating.

Children today enjoy making stick-jaw just as much as the French Huguenot children at the Cape enjoyed it, particularly if it entails collecting pine cones and knocking out the dennepitte *(pine-nut kernels).*

34 *Dennepitte* – pine kernels – are traditional ingredients of *tameletjie*, though almonds make a tasty substitute. The silver kettle-stand, with its beaded rim and graceful floral swags, was made in the mid-18th century by Johan Hendrik Vos, believed to be the earliest silversmith to serve his apprenticeship at the Cape.

Van der Hum liqueur

6 bottles of brandy (750 ml each)
80 g (12 tablespoons) naartje peel, cut into thin strips
A handful of orange blossoms
1 bottle of rum (750 ml)
36 cloves
1,5 nutmegs
6 sticks of cinnamon
A few cardamom seeds

Bruise the spices slightly, tie up in muslin cloth and place in an earthenware jar or small cask. Add the brandy, naartje peel and orange blossoms. Shake up every day for a month. Strain. Make a heavy syrup by boiling 1,5 kg sugar and 6 cups (1,5 l) water and allow to cool. Add the strained brandy mixture and the rum to the cold syrup. Allow the liqueur to stand for three weeks and decant into bottles. Cork and seal with wax.

Serve in liqueur glasses as a soetsopie.

According to one author, Admiral van der Hum of the V.O.C. fleet was so fond of the naartje-flavoured golden liqueur that his Cape friends named it after him. If the liqueur is too sweet for the uninitiated, add a little brandy to make 'brandy-hum'.

Small pancakes with Van der Hum

60 g (half cup) flour
1 ml (quarter teaspoon) salt
1 egg
125 ml (half cup) milk
125 ml (half cup) water
10 ml (1 dessertspoon) melted butter

Sift the flour and salt, mix into soft dough with beaten egg and small amounts of milk and water. Add the rest of the milk and water and beat briskly. Add the melted butter and allow to stand for an hour. Drop spoonsful onto greased hot pan. When they start to bubble, turn and cook until the other side is lightly browned. Roll up the pancakes and just before serving, pour Van der Hum liqueur over them.

Serve with thin cream.

For many generations children delighted in eating as titbits all sorts of wild plants that never found their way to the Cape table. Among these was baro (Cyphia digitata), a juicy, sweet corm rather like a small potato, and sweet wild-fennel roots (Chamarea capensis) were dug up and eaten as well. Children used to gather frutang, sometimes called 'knikkers' (Romulea longifolia), and plait and chew their long fruit-tipped stems, while bokhoring pods (Astephanus neglectus) were eaten and their pink flowers sucked for their sweet sap. They also eagerly collected golden-brown 'boetabessies' (Chrysanthemoides monilifera) so named because their three or five succulent fruit were clustered together like little brothers in a bed, and these as well as the drab-green taaibos berries (Rhus lucida) were eaten as a treat.

A certain species of protea was given the name 'sugarbush' (Protea repens). As this indicates, the calyx secretes a sweet nectar which was collected to make 'bossiestroop', a highly-prized delicacy among children. In fact, Lady Anne Barnard found the flavour so delectable that she sent some of the syrup home to her friends in England.

Sadly enough, it is no longer easy to find these edible wild plants

35 Pancakes laced with naartje-flavoured Van der Hum liqueur are a delectable dessert. The exquisite famille rose Chinese porcelain on which this dish is served is part of a dinner service – including custard cups – made for Rudolph Cloete of Constantia in c.1795. **36** Protea repens – the sugarbush and South African floral emblem – secretes a honey-sweet nectar which children collected to make 'bossiestroop'.

for they have become very scarce indeed and those that have survived should certainly be protected. It is difficult, too, to recognise them for over the years many of their names have changed. For instance, confusion has arisen because the early colonists sometimes named plants after varieties which they had known in Europe but which bear no relation to those growing at the Cape. In this way the various species of *Moraea edulis* came to be called *wilde ajuin* (wild onion), a name which changed in time to *ajuintjie* and then to *uintjie* and Kolbe, the 18th century botanist, complained with some justification that the bulb neither looked nor tasted in the least like an onion but was more like a potato. Among the names popularly given to the *Moraea* family were baboon, mountain, vlei, goat, thick-skinned, reed, Bushman and Hottentot *uintjies*. Other varieties of these plants have retained their original vernacular names but the interpretation given them often varies, as with *berroé*, *baroe* or *baroo*, all of which refer to *Cyphia digitata*. On the other hand different names were often given to the same plants – 'frutang' and 'knikkers' for example both refer to *Caesalpinia major*.

A revival of interest by both scientists and gourmets in these interesting edible wild plants could well result in their being cultivated for the modern Cape table.

37

37 The bulb of the *bloublommetjie-uintjie (Morea fugax)*, when peeled and sautéed in butter, has a pleasant chestnut-like flavour.

A TRADITIONAL TABLE

The culinary arts brought to the Cape by the Dutch, French and other population groups merged in the 18th century and a new form developed which had a character entirely of its own. Apart from edible wild plants such as *wateruintjies* which are found only in South Africa, all the ingredients and materials needed for a distinctive, traditional table at which could be served characteristic dishes which evolved at the Cape, are universally available.

CHAPTER FOUR

THE KITCHEN AND PANTRY

THE OLD CAPE KITCHEN

The old Cape kitchen, with its cheerful hearth, its cast-iron pots and kettles and its gleaming copper cauldrons was the scene of considerable creative activity. Here bread and pastry ready for baking were shovelled on long-handled peels into the oven beside the fire, and red-hot coals were piled on the lids of tart and patty pans to bake the favourite snacks that they contained.

The Cape's first kitchen was in Van Riebeeck's wattle and daub fort, and here ship's cooks prepared meals for everyone ashore. It was they who were responsible for the origin of a very important Afrikaans word, *kombuis,* for the Dutch seaman's term for a ship's galley was *combuijs* in contrast to the word *keuken* which

Milk soup
360 g (3 cups) flour
3 eggs
Pinch of salt
A little water
Make a stiff dough from the flour and other ingredients. Roll out very thinly and cut into long strips. Pack the strips on top of one another with a sprinkling of flour between strips. Cut cross-wise into thinner strips.

Boil approximately 8 cups (2 l) milk in a deep saucepan. Cook the noodles for about 15 minutes in the milk over low heat, shaking the pan from time to time to separate the noodles. Add 1 tablespoon (12,5 ml) butter and serve in soup plates. Sprinkle with cinnamon-sugar and serve.

This is usually served as an evening meal.

38 An illustration from an old Dutch cook book.

was used to denote a kitchen on land. But the kitchen at the fort inherited this nautical term, and very soon after his arrival we find Van Riebeeck himself referring to the *combuijs* when he recorded that it had been flooded in a storm.

In the houses built at the Cape the kitchen was placed at the end of a wing, so that the chimney could be supported by a gable. It provided an outlet for the smoke as it was built over the open fireplace which in larger buildings occupied the entire width of the kitchen so that quite a number of kettles, pans, pots and gridirons could be used at the same time.

Ovens were usually built next to the fireplace with the oven door overhanging the hearth so that the coals could be raked out onto the hearth floor. In smaller houses they were most often built outside the house near the back door. At first those in the house or in the yard had slate or wooden doors lined on the inside with a sheet of iron, but cast-iron oven doors made in Sweden were imported later via Holland. Special circumstances demanded ingenious substitutes and, for example, when people were on the move or their kitchens had not yet been built they made use of hollowed-out ant-heaps or holes in river-banks. Coals were placed inside these and they were then sealed with flat stones.

HOME INDUSTRY

In the days when the housewife was unable to buy bread, butter and meat she had to rely on her own kitchen and back-yard to provide food for the table. Hers was a busy life and she divided her week into days for baking, slaughtering, washing and ironing.

39

The dairy required her attention every day; cream had to be separated and, a few times a week, butter had to be churned. The fruit season was particularly demanding for there were jams, pickles and chutney to be cooked, vinegar to be made, fruit syrups and brandied fruits to be prepared, and fruit to be dried.

Winter's cooler weather was slaughtering time. Boerewors was made and the left-over fat rendered into soap, while the hard intestinal fat of sheep, goats and cattle was used to make candles. Dripping was stored in earthenware pots for later use, and the crackling enjoyed as a special treat.

BAKING DAY

In most Cape homes there were two baking days a week so that there was always fresh bread in the house.

Wheat, ground in watermills or windmills or even in primitive horse-mills, yielded a coarse whole-wheat flour. When a small quantity of flour was needed in the home it was ground in a handmill, colloquially called a '*gatskuurder*' (hole grinder) because of the hole in the millstone.

The flour was stored in a yellowwood flour-bin with four compartments: one for coarse flour, another for white flour, a third for sifted bran and a fourth for rye, barley and so on.

In the 18th century the Cape colonist generally ate white bread, while rye and barley bread was normally baked for the slaves.

Sweet yeast bread is peculiar to the Cape; the evening before baking day the yeast was prepared by mixing flour into a basin of lukewarm water and salt. Normally the flour was strewn in a circle starting from the outside and working inwards so that the outside layer was thicker than that at the centre. The basin was then covered with a lid, wrapped tightly in the breadcloth or bread-blanket and set to one side of the fireplace so that the heat would speed up the fermentation process. The next morning more flour was stirred in – a process referred to as '*oorsuur*' (over-leavening). Meanwhile the correct quantity of flour for the batch of bread was scooped into the yellowwood baking trough which stood at a convenient height on a yellowwood stand. A bay was made in the flour and into this the leavening was thrown and stirred until all the flour had been moistened. Now the kneading process began – and for this a strong pair of arms was necessary. The dough was worked with clenched fists and turned again and again until it was elastic and well-kneaded. After that it was patted smooth and covered with the bread-blanket to rise once again. After an hour or so it was ready to be shaped into loaves made by pinching off pieces of equal size which were rolled out on the flour-strewn lid of the baking trough. The unbaked loaves were allowed to rise for a while longer under the bread-blanket before baking. While this was going on *waboom* and grapevine stumps were used to heat the oven to the right temperature and here experience played an important part. As a general rule the temperature was correct for baking when you could hold your hand in the oven for a count of 13 before it became intolerable. Those not skilled at this hazardous practice could test the heat by placing a knob of dough in the oven and watching to see how long it took to turn brown.

Now the coals of the oven were raked out and the breadpans placed inside with a long-handled peel. An hour later the oven

Must bread

During the wine-making season it was the practice to use fresh must as a leavening agent, and must bread and mosbolletjies were baked.

2,5 kg flour
500 g sugar
10 ml (1 dessertspoon) aniseed
A little grated nutmeg
A little salt
125 g butter
1,25 ℓ must

Mix dry ingredients, rub in butter and knead with must. Leave to rise overnight in a warm place. Make into loaves the following morning, leave to rise again and bake for between one hour and 75 minutes in a hot oven (200° C).

Must buns (Mosbolletjies)

The dried bread used on board ship and known as ship's biscuit was sometimes baked with sugar instead of salt for a change, but it was not nearly as tasty as the must buns baked at the Cape and known as beskuit *when dried. When must was not available, the yeast was made from raisins.*

500 g raisins with seeds
5 kg sifted flour
1 kg sugar
10 ml (1 dessertspoon) salt
25 ml (2 tablespoons) aniseed
500 g butter or a mixture of butter and pork fat
2 eggs
Lukewarm milk or milk and water

Bruise the raisins, place in a jar and add 1 tablespoon (12,5 ml) sugar and approximately 6 cups (1,5 ℓ) water. Leave to stand in a warm place until all the raisins have risen to the surface (approx. two days) and strain the must.

Sift the flour, add the sugar, salt and aniseed, make a hollow in the middle of the flour and add the must. Sprinkle a little flour over the top and leave to rise for approximately one hour in a warm place.

Melt the butter, beat the eggs and add to the lukewarm milk. Knead all the remaining ingredients into the flour. Knead until the dough is firm, spread a little butter over the top and leave to rise overnight. Make into buns the following morning and pack close together in pans. Leave to rise until they double in height, brush a little milk over the top and bake for approximately an hour in a hot oven (200° C). Remove, break apart and dry in a slow oven (140° C).

39 A housewife uses a wooden *wasbalie* on washing day. *Balies* – teak barrels with brass or iron hoops – were made in many shapes and sizes and served various purposes from pickling and butter-making to foot-washing.

Cracknels

Take risen must bun dough, cut into thin strips and mould in the shape of figure eights. Brush with melted butter and sprinkle with castor sugar. Place cracknels separately in flat pans and bake in a hot oven (200° C) for about 20 minutes.

Cracknel makes a crackling noise between the teeth and this has given it its name. It was the first pastry offered for sale at the Cape by the free bakers under Commander van Riebeeck. The original recipe is a bread recipe made with sifted flour.

Tempies

Take risen must bun dough, shape into small buns and pack them separately in a flat pan. Press a raisin into each one, brush with milk and egg beaten together and bake in a hot oven (200° C). Eat fresh.

The following little poem about this early delicacy, translated from the Afrikanerized Dutch, comes from Tulbagh:

> *'If it's beer and buns you wish to buy*
> *Martjie's shop is the one to try.*
> *Those of Meintjie are sour, I fear*
> *And worse still they are awfully dear.'*

(The Martjie of the poem was a master baker with her own small bakery.)

40 In wheat-growing areas the smooth circular threshing floor with its low surrounding wall was an essential part of every farmstead. Sjambok in hand, a man drives the galloping horses over sheaves of corn spread out three layers deep, while his companion turns the hay with a fork.

door was opened and if the loaves were a crisp golden brown they were taken out with a curved iron rabble. The bread tins were then turned upside down on the flat platform of the oven or onto a table or the lid of the bread bin and the loaves shaken out to cool.

In the days before the introduction of greased baking tins, round pieces of dough were simply placed on the oven floor. This so-called 'floor bread' was usually covered with ash which had to be scraped off with a piece of wood.

The delicious smell of freshly baked bread whetted everyone's appetite, but since warm loaves could not be cut immediately a piece of left-over dough was sometimes made into *vetkoek*. These small balls of dough were left to rise for a while and then fried in a pan of dripping until crisp and brown. Quick to make and satisfying, they were eaten while the other loaves were cooling off. If bread was needed at short notice, pot bread was made by baking the dough in a pot over the coals in the fireplace or in a hole in the ground.

There were several types of bread at the time; for instance, bread dough was sometimes shaped into balls and cooked like dumplings with the simmering meat. This 'pot bread' was eaten with gravy and tasted exactly like fresh bread. 'Ash bread' or 'ash cake' was simply baked on the coals or was buried under the ashes where it took longer. 'Gridiron cakes' eaten on slaughtering days,

---

Raisin bread

1 kg white flour
250 g sugar
150 g raisins
60 g butter
Ground cinnamon
Grated nutmeg
10 ml (1 dessertspoon) ground aniseed
500 ml (2 cups) must

Mix dry ingredients, rub in butter and knead with two cups (500 ml) must. Leave to rise and bake for one hour in a hot oven (200° C).

This was a special delicacy for children and with many families it was the custom to include a raisin loaf in the koskis *on the horsecab or coach for the children to nibble on during the journey. It was also served as a substitute for cake.*

Dumpling soup

Make a soup from:
1 kg beef
2 mace leaves
2,5 – 3,5 ℓ (8-12 cups) water
6 cloves
1 spray of sorrel
Salt to taste

To make the dumplings, melt one tablespoon (12,5 ml) soft fat or butter in one cup (250 ml) boiling water and thicken with two cups (250 g) flour. Allow to cool, fold in two eggs and shape into dumplings the size of walnuts. Steam the dumplings in the soup.

---

41 An old *koringharp* from a farm near Bredasdorp. This was a type of sieve specially made for the removal of weevils which often infested grain after it had been stored for a long time. **42** Baking was developed to a fine art and the housewife prided herself on the variety as well as the quality of the breads she made. The oven, set at the end of the open hearth, was fed with *waboom* branches and grapevine stumps, and once the correct temperature was reached – the skilled baker used her bare hand to assess this – the coals were raked away to make way for the risen dough.

were baked on the gridiron after the liver, kidneys, thick intestine and other delicacies had been grilled on it for breakfast – a meal to think of with nostalgia in these days of continental breakfasts.

Some breads were special delicacies and raisin bread for instance was baked during the grape-harvesting season when fresh must was available with which to leaven the dough. Later during the 19th century when farmers from the interior introduced maize to the Cape kitchen, maize bread made its appearance as well.

Mention should also be made of *kluitjies* or dumplings, which were often eaten as a kind of bread. The flour, egg and milk batter is thinner than bread dough and it is prepared by ladling spoonfuls of the mixture into a pot of boiling water or some other liquid. Dumpling pudding is well known, but dumplings were also steamed in stews or in soups – the perfect meal for a cold wet winter's day in the Boland.

SLAUGHTERING DAY

After the initial shortage of meat in Van Riebeeck's time, more and more meat appeared on the Cape table until in the 18th century it had virtually become the staple food. And households that did not buy their supplies from the local butchers, did their own slaughtering at least once a week.

The carefully selected sheep or goat was slaughtered by a special 'slagjong' or butcher who was a good hand at it. He slit the animal's throat with a butcher's knife and left it to bleed. The blood was sometimes collected for dishes such as black-pudding or black soup, and mixed with gall it was also used to smear on floors to give them a bright glossy finish.

After the slaughtered animal had been bled, the hide was slit open along the chest and stomach and carefully removed from the carcase so that it did not get covered in fat or hair. The intestinal fat, called caul, or long fat, was later rendered into hard fat, the entrails were removed and the heart, liver and kidneys cooked and eaten. Less palatable parts such as the spleen and lungs, also known as the 'pluck', were sometimes cleaned and minced to make hash. And, as a special treat, the tail of the sheep or goat, as well as the chitterlings – the lowest part of the colon – were grilled.

The skinned carcase was hung up by the hind legs on a meat hook and, after it had cooled off, it was cut up neatly into eight pieces: the hind legs, the fore legs, two ribs, the chine and the neck. These cuts were lightly salted and left to hang overnight to be wind-dried by the cool night air. In the morning they were placed in a bag or wrapped in linen and stored in a cool place. The meat was then hung out regularly every evening on a meat crown consisting of a round hoop with hooks on which pieces of meat were suspended, until it had been used up.

The fat tails of sheep together with other surplus fat were rendered for household use. The pure white mutton fat was a special delicacy spread on fresh bread, gridiron cakes or ash cakes, particularly if eaten with preserves such as that made from watermelon, or the slightly tart apricot jam.

Cleanliness was extremely important in the preparation of offal and the head, tripe and trotters of the slaughtered sheep carcase deserve special mention. The tripe was washed very thoroughly both inside and out and then scraped. Once clean it was cut up

Sausage

Every sausage-maker has a favourite recipe. The following are well-tried old recipes:

Pork sausage

5 kg minced pork, half fat and half lean
5 ml (1 teaspoon) thyme
5 ml (1 teaspoon) sage
5 ml (1 teaspoon) ground nutmeg
5 ml (1 teaspoon) allspice
5 ml (1 teaspoon) mace
12,5 ml (1 tablespoon) ground coriander
20 g (1,5 tablespoons) salt
30 g (2 tablespoons) ground pepper
Half bottle of red wine
Mix the meat with all the spices. Then mix well with the wine and stuff the mixture into a sausage casing, using a sausage stuffer.

Boerewors (Mixed Meats)

1,5 kg pork
1,5 kg beef or mutton
500 g speck
1 nutmeg, grated
Rind of 1 orange, finely chopped
12 sage leaves
10 ml (2 teaspoons) pepper
20 g (4 teaspoons) salt
12,5 ml (1 tablespoon) ground coriander
5 ml (1 teaspoon) marjoram
Mince the meat together. (In the old days the meat was cubed.) Add all the other ingredients, mix well and fill sausage casing.

Beef sausage

4 kg beef
1,25 – 1,5 kg beef fat
12,5 ml (1 tablespoon) ground pimento
Salt and pepper
5 ml (1 teaspoon) ground cloves
37,5 ml (3 tablespoons) ground coriander
Mince the meat and cut the fat into cubes. Add the other ingredients, mix well and fill the sausage casing.

43 Every farmer had his favourite recipe for boerewors. Before the introduction of the *worsstopper*, or sausage machine, funnels made of cow-horn or tin were used and sausage casings were made from the preserved intestines of sheep or goats. The chopped meat was pressed into the *worsstopper* with a cylindrical stinkwood mallet.

finely and cooked with the head and trotters. These were first soaked in boiling water to loosen the hair before they were carefully scraped. The head, snout included, was slit open with an axe and all the glands and impurities removed; it was then washed meticulously. The nasal bone was usually set aside for the yard dog to gnaw.

The eyes, brains and tongue were tender and the choicest fare. Children clamoured for the knuckle-bones of the trotters which they ate clean and sucked dry to play with as toy horses, oxen, *tou leiers* and so on. Cold offal, set in its own jelly, or curried, was a regular favourite. In some households roasted sheep's head was prepared for the table by burying it under hot ashes to cook slowly.

Winter was the main slaughtering time and such occasions were usually festive ones when neighbours came over to lend a hand. Oxen and pigs were specially fattened and the housewife made sure that there were enough spices in the house to season the meat. Perhaps the hardest work was to make the endless strings of boerewors and for this washed pig intestines were used as sausage casings because they were the correct thickness. The most popular recipe for boerewors called for a mixture of pork, beef and cubes of speck, flavoured with salt, pepper and a variety of spices, especially coriander. Fresh boerewors was a favourite breakfast or evening grill.

Before mincing machines came into use during the 19th century the meat was chopped fine or 'hashed' with a large meat knife on the so-called *hackebord*. Sheep and goat intestines were collected during the year as casings for thin sausage which had to be dried

Meat dishes from offal
Apart from tripe-and-trotters, other traditional dishes are also made from offal.

Haksel
Cook the pluck (lungs, heart and trachea) of a sheep until soft and then mince. To the meat and kooknat (juices left in the pot after the meat has been cooked), add:

1 onion, chopped
12,5 ml (1 tablespoon) vinegar
5 ml (1 teaspoon) salt
1 thick slice of bread

Bring to the boil and simmer, stirring all the time, until pulpy and serve as a main dish, or with bread for breakfast or supper.

Liver in caul fat (also called vlermuis, muis *and* skilpad)

1 sheep's liver, minced
1 slice of white bread, soaked in milk
75 g currants
Salt, pepper and grated nutmeg
1 egg
1 onion, finely chopped
25 ml (2 tablespoons) vinegar
250 g – 375 g caul fat (meaty casing of fat surrounding sheep's stomach)

Mix all ingredients and spoon into the caul fat which has been spread out in a baking pan. Fold closed and secure with skewers. Pour a little water into the baking pan and bake for approx. one hour in a medium oven (180° C) until well browned, basting occasionally.

rapidly. The intestine was pulled over the point of the sausage stuffer which worked on the principle of a funnel. At first cow-horn or tin funnels were used but in the 19th century iron ones were introduced. A knot was made at one end of the intestine so that the meat could not be squeezed out, and in this way long strings of sausage were made. Dried sausage was in fact one of the best ways of preserving meat, but there were other methods such as wind-drying for beef, pork and venison.

A special Afrikaans custom was associated with a major slaughtering day: the sending of *'karmenaadjies'* or gifts of meat to neighbours. Such a gift packet, normally consisting of one of the better cuts of meat, a piece of speck and a length of sausage, was sent as a token of good neighbourliness or friendship – a gesture that was always appreciated.

THE PRESERVATION OF FOOD

The Cape housewife in the early days had to plan carefully to ensure that she stored enough food for her household and at the same time prevented it from spoiling so that she had fresh produce always available for later use. Otto Mentzel, who became well acquainted with Cape customs during the eight years he spent here, noted that Cape housewives were very fussy about the quality of their food; fresh meat more than three days old was simply not used. However, the hot southern summers made it very difficult to preserve meat and the housewives developed various processes to a fine art.

Spices and herbs, sugar, salt and vinegar were skilfully applied

Brawn

2 pork trotters
1,5 kg shin
5 ml (1 teaspoon) pepper
4 cloves
4 whole pimentos
12,5 (1 tablespoon) salt
62,5 ml (quarter cup) vinegar
1 bayleaf

Singe and scrape off all hair and bristles. Make a slit from between the trotters as far as the first joint. Remove gland from between trotters. Saw bones into smaller pieces. Cover the trotters with water, add all the other ingredients and simmer until the meat comes away from the bones (approximately five hours or about one and a half hours in pressure-cooker) and a small quantity of liquid is left. Remove the bones and cut meat into small pieces. Pour into wetted moulds and allow to set. Serve slices of cold brawn with salad such as slaphakskeen-tjies *(cooked onion salad) or tomato salad.*

44 Judging from their size, the steaks smoking over the open fire must have been obtained from the elephant shot by François le Vaillant during his famous expedition at the end of the 18th century.

Jam and preserves
(In the old days, called comfits)

General
Choice of fruit: *Select fresh fruit without bruises or blemishes and of approximately the same size. A mixture of ripe and slightly green fruit usually gives the best jam and preserves.*
Preparation of fruit: *Every variety is prepared in a different way according to the recipe: grating, peeling, pricking or removing the pith or pips. Boil the fruit in water and as soon as it is soft, place it in boiling syrup. Add the fruit a little at a time to ensure that the syrup does not come off the boil.*

If fruit is very sweet or overripe, add a little lemon juice before the syrup begins to boil. This will prevent crystallization.

The syrup
For most kinds of fruit the proportions are 500 g sugar to 500 g fruit (that is, a 1 to 1 ratio) but for soft fruit the proportions are 375 g sugar to 500 g fruit (that is, a 3 to 4 ratio).

For fruit that has to cook for a long time (such as watermelon rind or citrus), use 750 ml to 1 ℓ (3 to 4 cups) water for 500 g sugar. In the case of pulpy fruit such as tomatoes or berries, use 250 ml to 500 ml (1 to 2 cups) water for 500 g sugar.

Firm fruit should be cooked in a thinner syrup because thick syrup draws out the juice and causes the fruit to shrink. There should be enough syrup to cover the fruit when it is bottled.

Stir the syrup and do not allow it to boil until all the sugar has been dissolved.

Cooking of fruit in the syrup
Use a large heavy-bottomed saucepan. It must never be more than half filled with fruit.

First, boil the fruit in water until tender but not soft. It is ready as soon as it can easily be pierced with a match. Spoon one piece at a time into boiling syrup, ensuring that the syrup does not come off the boil. Then boil the fruit rapidly in an open saucepan, skimming off the scum. Boil until the fruit is clear and the syrup is of the right consistency. Test the consistency of the syrup in the following way:

Skim off a little syrup, allow to cool slightly and then allow to drip off the spoon.

If the jam or preserve is ready, the syrup of fruits containing a large quantity of fruit jelly, such as citrus, will drip off the spoon in large globules. In the case of other fruits such as green figs or watermelon pieces, the syrup will run off slowly in a thick stream. If the syrup is of the correct consistency before the fruit is clear and well cooked, make and add a thin syrup. If the syrup is too thin and the fruit is already well cooked, remove the fruit and boil the syrup separately to the correct consistency. Then add the fruit and boil thoroughly.

to prevent the meat from going off, and each household had a pickling vat in which meat was stored. It contained a strong solution of salt, saltpetre and brown sugar, in which pork, beef or mutton could be preserved for considerable lengths of time provided the meat was turned every day, was covered entirely by the solution and the vat kept tightly covered. Ginger, cloves, pimento, peppercorns and mace provided additional flavouring. When the meat was taken out to be cooked it was first boiled in fresh water and this liquid was set aside so that any cooked meat remaining after the meal could be preserved a while longer by being kept in the liquid.

A Cape delicacy, 'tassal meat', was made by cutting out the tender flesh along the chine of a pig or buck, salting it, rubbing it lightly with pepper and scorched coriander and then covering it with vinegar. In this way it could be preserved for a few weeks. Before it was cooked, it was rinsed in water and then pan-fried.

Venison and the tender cuts of beef could be preserved for several days in a mixture of wine and/or vinegar, brown sugar, whole cloves, peppercorns and herbs such as thyme, laurel leaves, rosemary or other flavourings according to family taste. The meat was rubbed well with dried spices, including ground cloves, pepper, pimento (allspice) and then steeped in the wine or vinegar mixture in a covered tub. It was turned daily and when this tasty cut was prepared for the table it was usually larded with pieces of speck, and then pot-roasted or stewed with spices until tender and juicy.

Out of this practice of preserving meat with salt, vinegar and spices, the method of making biltong developed. The so-called thick flank of a buck or beef carcase was cut neatly, along the grain of the muscles and tendons, into strips which were then rubbed with salt, dried spices and saltpetre and sprinkled with vinegar. After a day or two the biltong was hung up to become wind-dry and sometimes it was even placed in the chimney to speed up the drying process. It may take a month or so to become properly dry and, because mould develops quickly during the damp Boland winter, biltong was more often made in the drier regions where the cattle and trek farmers lived.

Smoking meat in the chimney not only preserved it but actually enhanced its flavour. In old Cape documents there are many references to 'Cape ham' and, in 1705, Adam Tas sent one to a funeral meal. A century later Lady Anne Barnard included two such hams in her provisions for a journey to Stellenbosch and the interior and, according to Otto Mentzel, Cape ham was as good as that of Hamburg. It was made by leaving a leg of pork in brine for about a month after which the surplus fluid was squeezed out and the leg smoked in the chimney for a further three weeks. By subsequently storing it in a cool place it could be kept for several months until needed. Beautiful cauldrons made of copper were used to cook the hams.

Brawn, made by boiling up the cleaned and scraped trotters of animals and allowing the jelly to set after pieces of cooked meat, spices and herbs had been added could also be kept for a while and on hot summer days this palatable cold meat went down very well.

Fish caught in Cape waters were preserved in three ways: by smoking, salting or drying. Snoek, in particular, was smoked while mullet was hung up, preferably in warm weather, to dry.

Another method was to cook the fish and then pickle it in a mixture of vinegar, onions and spices, and most varieties were preserved in this way, but snoek and steenbras were preferred. Mullet was pickled according to the Dutch recipe for making pickled herring.

Besides meat and fish the housewife kept a supply of provisions that could be used for *toekos*, or side dishes, which were served with meat and fish. In addition, certain vegetables such as pumpkin and dried beans, and grains such as rice and wheat, could be stored.

Fresh fruit such as quinces, apples and pears, for instance, was packed in straw and stored for several months in a cool place – usually the loft – and the family coffins that were kept there were sometimes used as storage places. Fruit was also dried and then kept for long periods.

Fruit was preserved as well, but not by the modern method of boiling in sugar and water and sterilizing. It was only in 1795 that the Frenchman, Nikolaas Appert, discovered that food which had been heated in sealed containers could be kept for a long time – provided the containers were not opened.

Initially salt was the preservative, and Cape fruit such as quinces – a well known local speciality – was most probably preserved in this way, just as salt was used to pickle green beans, too. 'Cape mebos' was the name given to dried apricots preserved with salt according to the Eastern method of preparing '*mebos*' – which was in fact salted plums. Old documents claim that these preserved plums were made at the Cape, too, and they reveal that women chewed salted fruit as a cure for morning sickness.

The jars of preserved mulberries, grapes and other deciduous fruit mentioned in old records were presumably earthenware, and the fruit itself was preserved in brandy. These '*soetsopies*', or brandied fruits, were offered to guests on cold winter evenings.

STORAGE

THE LOFT AND LOFT CUPBOARD

The loft above the reed or timber ceiling of the early Cape houses was cool and perfectly suited as a storage place for food. Below it, next to the chimney where it became narrower, there was a cupboard kept warm and dry by the heat of the chimney. Here food such as biltong and dried fruit which had to be protected from moisture was stored. There was a great variety of dried fruit, including raisins, apricots, peaches, pears, quinces, apples and figs, as well as locally grown nuts such as almonds, used in many old recipes. Plaited strings of onions or bunches of dried fish were hung from the collar-beams – the open beams in the roof of the house – to keep dry.

THE FOOD CUPBOARD

More valuable commodities such as tea and sugar were stored in the food cupboard, which was usually made of yellowwood, or stinkwood with yellowwood panels. Very few examples remain and today they are treasured items in museums and private collections.

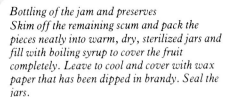

Bottling of the jam and preserves
Skim off the remaining scum and pack the pieces neatly into warm, dry, sterilized jars and fill with boiling syrup to cover the fruit completely. Leave to cool and cover with wax paper that has been dipped in brandy. Seal the jars.
   Allowing jam to cool in the saucepan will prevent shrinkage of the fruit. Jam cooled in this way must be packed into clean jars, sealed airtight and sterilized in boiling water for 15 minutes. Then seal thoroughly.
   Store jam in a cool dry dark place. In the past jam was stored in earthenware jars, with dried ox-bladders tied over the tops to seal them.

Watermelon preserve
Cut into slices approximately 50 mm thick, cut off the soft flesh and the green outer skin and use the rind. Prick each slice with a fork and cut into oblong or square pieces. Weigh.
   Steep the pieces overnight (tsamma, *wild watermelon, must be steeped for two days) in a solution of two tablespoons (25 ml) slaked lime per 14 cups (3,5 ℓ) water. Drain, rinse and leave to soak for two hours in clean water. Boil the rind in water until tender.
   Make a syrup of 500 g sugar for every 500 g fruit and use three to four cups (750 ml – 1 ℓ) water for every 500 g sugar. Add three tablespoons (37,5 ml) lemon juice to every kilogram of fruit.
   Boil the pieces in syrup until the fruit is translucent and the syrup of the right heavy consistency. Drain, pack into sterilized jars, fill with syrup and seal.

Gherkin preserve (agurkiekonfyt)
Use the basic syrup for watermelon preserve. Prick the gherkins well with a darning needle and soak overnight in salt water: 1 tablespoon (12,5 ml) salt in 2,5 ℓ water. Drain off all the water and press cloves into a few gherkins.
   Boil the gherkins in the syrup, skim off the scum and bottle as explained above.

Green tomato preserve
Choose unblemished tomatoes of uniform size. Prick the skins with a darning needle or fork and soak overnight in a salt solution: 1 tablespoon (12,5 ml) salt to 2,5 ℓ water. Rinse tomatoes well and weigh.
   Prepare a syrup of 500 g sugar for every 500 g tomatoes and 1 cup (250 ml) water for every 3 cups (750 g) sugar. A few pieces of bruised ginger may be added to the syrup for flavour. Add the tomatoes to the boiling syrup and boil briskly until the syrup is thick. Bottle and seal.

Green fig preserve

Use the basic syrup recipe for watermelon preserve (p. 69). The figs must be plump but not hollow. The peel is scraped, peeled or grated off very thinly. Leave the stalks intact and make an incision in the form of a cross at the rounded end of the fig. Weigh the figs. Soak overnight in lime water (see under watermelon preserve) and rinse.

Boil the figs, together with a few young fig leaves, until tender – approx. 15 minutes. Whole ginger or cloves may be added. Place the figs in the boiling syrup and boil quite briskly until they are translucent. If the syrup has not reached the required consistency, spoon out the figs and cook the syrup until thick enough. Then add the fruit to the syrup and boil until done. Bottle as explained (p. 69).

Sour fig jam

Use the same syrup as for green fig preserve.

Leave the ripe, dried sour figs to soak in boiling water until the skins are soft. Remove the hard bottom sections of the fruit and cook until tender. Place in boiling syrup and cook until it is the consistency of jam and dark in colour.

Grape jam ('Korrelkonfyt')

This jam is usually made from Hanepoot grapes. Wash the grapes. Remove the seeds if you wish. Then steam the grapes for 10 minutes to soften the skins. Spoon the grapes out of the water, allow to cool and weigh. Using 375 g sugar for every 500 g fruit, arrange the fruit and the sugar in layers in a heavy-bottomed saucepan. Leave on the side of the stove until the juice is partly drawn out and the fruit and sugar slightly warm. Then heat slowly, stirring occasionally until all the sugar is dissolved: make sure that the syrup does not boil before all the sugar is dissolved. Boil briskly until the fruit is clear and translucent and the syrup is thick. Bottle and seal.

In the old days grape jam was flavoured with aniseed. Tie 1 teaspoon (5 ml) aniseed in a muslin bag, put the bag in the saucepan at the beginning of the jam-making and remove before bottling.

THE PANTRY

The word *dispens* originated in 17th century seaman's vernacular and originally meant simply the place where food was stored. Until the beginning of the 19th century this term appears in old writings, but it was eventually abbreviated in everyday speech to 'spens' (pantry) and became the name for the separate room, adjoining the kitchen, in which foodstuffs, cooking utensils and dinnerware were stored. This separate room first appeared in buildings towards the middle of the 18th century and usually contained yellowwood shelves above yellowwood cupboards.

Joachim von Dessin's inventory of his pantry in 1754, when the *dispens* was still a novelty in well-to-do Cape households, is revealing. He was secretary to the Orphan Chamber during the terms of office of governors Swellengrebel and Ryk Tulbagh, and his estate included an exceptional collection of books which later formed the nucleus of the present-day South African Library. His personal writings consisted of a *Briefboek* of his private letters, and his *Memoriaal* in which he recorded everyday events. The latter presents an excellent picture of the way of life at the Cape at that time. According to entries in this journal the following were to be found in his pantry: six hams; 200 pounds of salted beef; 150 pounds of salted speck; 150 pounds of dripping and 80 pounds of butter. *Toekos* included 13 muids of wheat; two muids of flour; one and a half muids of green peas; one and a half muids of yellow peas; one and half muids of white beans; two thirds of a muid of broad beans; 250 pounds of barley; 100 pounds of rice; brown beans; black beans; Madagascar beans; princess beans, sago and groats. His pantry also contained 274 pounds of coffee beans, 34 pounds of castor sugar, and 150 pounds of lump sugar or *theezuiker* also known as *klontgezuiker* – sugar cubes which were kept in the mouth while tea was being drunk.

The spices he records include 38 pounds of black pepper, seven pounds of white pepper and 31 pounds of tamarind, coriander, mustard and cumin seed and assorted others. He then lists a few luxury items: one pound of white bird's nests (for making soup), one small sack of Japanese rice and seven bottles of English olives pickled in brine. There were, in addition, 18 pounds of currants, 6 000 almonds, preserved plums, a half-aum of coconut oil, a *bierpijp* of white vinegar, 100 tallow candles, 220 pounds of hard soap, six loads of kindling and 400 bottles of imported and Cape wine.

Some food was not included on the inventory; Von Dessin mentions elsewhere that he had a supply of cumin cheese and sweetmilk cheese, and that he had bought mullet for making pickled herring, and steenbras for making pickled fish. In addition he made smoked sausage. His supply of dried fruit included figs, apricots, raisins and pears and he had ginger preserve and preserved mulberries on his shelves.

Food was usually kept in bulk because of the irregularity of supply ships at the Cape, but additional stocks could be bought locally in large quantities from private citizens, merchants or from the Company store.

Standard measures were the pound weight (0,45 kg), the muid (54 kg), the leaguer (582 litres) and the aum. An aum of wine or vinegar measured 155,25 litres and an aum of oil equalled 145,25 litres. The keg measure was generally used because wooden vats were the commonly used containers for the packing and shipping of various kinds of food. A butter keg weighed 17 kilograms, and butter, which had been well salted to preserve it, was still being imported in this way during the 19th century. An empty beer keg was frequently used as a measure for vinegar or other fluids and was referred to as a *bierpijp* in contemporary documents. Since people often had to borrow from one another, a pail became the usual measure for this purpose, eight pails equalling one muid.

Prices of various items are also indicated on old records. Most interesting of all these is Johanna Duminy's cash-book in which she recorded her expenses between the years 1790 and 1795 in unmistakably Afrikanerised Dutch. She was an educated Afrikaner woman and extracts from her cash-book reveal some of her purchases:

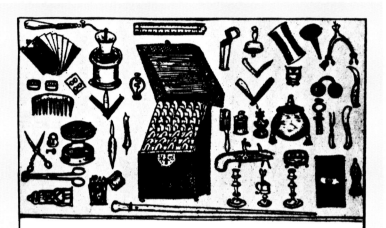

Rix (dollars)		Rix (dollars)	
2 thousand almonds	1	2 hams	6
1 muid of onions	1	one sucking pig	1
for 50 pounds of fat	5	1 cheese	3
100 pounds of soap	12	for 12 ducks	4
2 loads of wood	6	9 turkeys bought	9
1 half-aum brandy	6	1 small box of tea	4
1 half-aum of red		4 pounds of tea	3
pontac wine	10	100 pounds of coffee-	
2 leaguers of wine	46	beans	25
4 leaguers of wine	120	25 pounds raisins	8

2 leaguers of alberta wine at 20 rixdollars each and 6 rixdollars quitrent (to Company)	46
to the chief baker for bread delivered for a year	360
to rensburgh jansen for butter	360

Guilders and rixdollars were common currency at the Cape in the 18th century. A Cape guilder was worth 16 stuivers, while in Holland it was worth 20 stuivers. The Cape rixdollar was equal to 48 stuivers and a Cape stuiver was the equivalent of an English penny of the time.

Green apricot jam

Prick the apricots with a darning needle and soak overnight in a salt solution: 2 tablespoons salt (25 ml) in 3,5 ℓ water). Rinse in fresh water, weigh and cook in boiling water until soft.

Prepare a syrup of 500 g for 500 g fruit and 2 cups (500 ml) water for every 500 g sugar. Cook the fruit until it is translucent and the syrup thick. Bottle and seal.

Meboskonfyt (Sugared Mebos)

This traditional delicacy is not the same as the ordinary jams. Place ripe apricots in salt water and soak for three or four hours until the skin can be removed easily. Drain and lay the fruit on boards to dry in the sun. Turn the fruit over. On the third day squeeze the fruit gently to squeeze out the stone. Press the fruit flat. Soak in lime water for five minutes (see watermelon preserve p. 69). Remove and dry the fruit with a soft cloth. Rub white sugar well into each apricot: 750 g sugar for every 500 g fruit. Pack into jars with plenty of sugar between the layers and keep tightly covered.

To make jam from the mebos, soak in boiling water for a few hours and then drop one piece at a time into boiling syrup. (500 g sugar for 375 ml water). Boil until thick, bottle at once, and seal.

This Afrikaans folk-song recalls the old days:

> *'Aunt Mina boils the syrup*
> *For the Mebos konfyt*
> *From Wellington sugar*
> *At threepence a pound.'*

Naartje preserve

Citrus fruit may be soaked in fresh or salt water, but salt water may cause the rind to become tough if left for too long.

Grate the naartje peel off thinly, make a cross in the top and remove the pips with a small, sharp knife. Weigh and soak in water for two days, replacing the water twice with fresh water. Drain and plunge the naartjes into boiling water. Cook until the rind is so soft that it can easily be pierced with a matchstick.

Prepare syrup as for watermelon preserve (p. 69). Place the naartjes in the boiling syrup and boil rapidly until the fruit is translucent and the syrup thick. (See general instructions for the cooking of fruit in syrup if the syrup is too thick or too thin: p. 68).

Skim off and pack the naartjes neatly into sterilized jars. Fill with syrup and seal.

Seville orange preserve

Use the recipe for naartje preserve but after grating off the peel, rub the oranges with salt and leave to stand for 30 minutes. Pour boiling water over oranges, leave to stand until the water has cooled and rinse. Soak overnight in cold water.

The oranges may be used whole or cut into halves. Pack orange halves with the flat surface facing the outside of the jar to give an attractive appearance.

Citron preserve

Use the same syrup as for watermelon preserve (p. 69). The fruit must be plump but the peel must still be green.

Grate off the peel, or peel the fruit very thinly and cut the citrons into quarters. Remove the flesh. Only the rinds are used for preserves. Soak rinds for two days in fresh water, replacing the water at least once.

Cook further as for naartje preserve.

45 Jan van Riebeeck and his family would have been familiar with the strict etiquette observed at a meal such as this one in 17th century Europe. Hands are folded and men's hats removed during grace and, while adults are comfortably seated, the children are obliged to stand. **46** There were no fewer than 1 162 citrus trees at the Cape when Jan van Riebeeck completed his ten-year spell as Commander. Resourceful housewives converted the fruit into jams and jellies, and here citron preserve simmers in a gleaming copper saucepan supported over the embers by a wrought-iron trivet. Copper saucepans such as this one are still used for jam-making and enhance the green colour of certain preserves.

CHAPTER FIVE
TABLE MANNERS AND SOCIAL CUSTOMS

THE TABLE AND ETIQUETTE

Van Riebeeck's instructions that pewter plates and cups, knives and spoons, table-cloths and table napkins from the ship's stores were to be taken ashore give some indication of how the table was set for the first meals at the Cape.

During this period the upper classes ate off pewter plates while the poorer people used home-made wooden trenchers. Plates and drinking-cups made of pewter and in use during the settlement's early years are extremely scarce today for they were largely melted down to make bullets in times of emergency.

The table napkin was used in Van Riebeeck's period to wipe the hands and fingers as forks were not yet used. Etiquette demanded that the fingers be dipped into the common meat dish only as far as the first joint, and the food then conveyed to the mouth with no more than three fingers. Knives were commonly used for cutting meat while spoons were for so-called *lepelkos* (spoon food). Adults were seated at the table while the children stood beside it, and the men wore their hats throughout the meal, only removing them while grace was being said. According to the notes of Swedish botanist Sparrman who visited the Cape in 1772, this custom continued into the 18th century.

45

Dining-tables were of various shapes and sizes though at the Cape the rectangular design, made from local timber, was most frequently used. Carpenters preferred to fashion long, elegant family tables with yellowwood tops and stinkwood legs; sometimes round tables were made, but oval ones were a rarity.

Roast sucking pig

A sucking pig with an orange in its mouth was traditionally served at wedding receptions. The wedding feast was a splendid occasion held at the home of the bride.

Clean the sucking pig thoroughly and sprinkle the body cavity well with salt and fill with stuffing. Twist the front legs backwards, the hind legs forward, and fix with meat skewers. Rub the sucking pig with butter and wrap in greased brown or wax paper. Place in a roasting pan with water and roast in a hot oven (200° C) for about two and a half hours.

Remove the paper and continue roasting until brown, constantly brushing the surface with melted butter. Place a potato, apple or orange in the mouth and serve on a platter.

Stuffing
500 ml (2 cups) minced meat
25 ml (2 tablespoons) minced ham
7 ml (1,5 teaspoons) coriander
1 thick slice of bread soaked in milk
2 ml (half teaspoon) pounded cloves
Salt and pepper
12,5 ml (1 tablespoon) vinegar
1 egg
Mix all ingredients and use for stuffing the pig.

47 Fine blue and white Nanking porcelain, elegantly wrought silver, gleaming brass candlesticks and candelabra, and long-stemmed European wine glasses grace a table set for a wedding banquet. It was the custom to present all the courses simultaneously: roast sucking pig, chicken pie, roast duck, yellow rice with raisins, apple sambal, watercress salad and blancmange for dessert.

Over the years, as porcelain from the East was introduced and silversmiths applied their skills to the manufacture of tableware, eating utensils became increasingly elegant. In Europe the art of creating fine porcelain was mastered only at a much later stage. During the 18th Century, when shiploads of porcelain were regularly brought to Europe from China and Japan along the Cape sea-route, many of the pieces were eagerly intercepted by the burghers at the Cape and beautiful porcelain began to grace their voorkamers and dining-tables. The Company subsequently ordered its own design which featured the VOC monogram and this was used at the Castle and official residences.

48

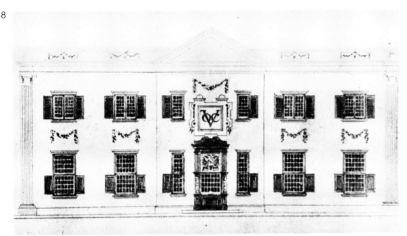

Then, gradually, as the lifestyle at the Cape became more sophisticated, the burghers followed the Company's example by ordering from the East their own personal dinner-services embossed with their family arms and monograms. Chinese Lowestoft from the *Tshin Lung* period (1736–1785), embellished with the *famille-rose* design of peach branches in full bloom, as well as blue-and-white Imperial porcelain of the *K'ang Hsi* period (1662–1722), were extremely popular. Imari– so-called 'Japaneseware' – manufactured on the mountain slopes in the Japanese province of Hizen, was also imported while the well-known Delftware, which later became a collector's item, was manufactured in imitation of the blue-and-white Eastern pattern.

From details given in old estate inventories it is possible to obtain an idea of how tables were set at the Cape at the beginning of the 18th century. At that time most tableware was made from pewter and in 1714, 36 pewter plates, beakers and dishes were itemized in an estate inventory, while the only porcelain mentioned was one butter dish, six platters, one set of 'pots' – presumably vases – and three figurines. Another inventory, dated 1760, on the other hand, makes no mention at all of pewter plates, although it records that on four shelves in the kitchen there were 30 plates, nine dishes, three basins and one beaker, all of porcelain.

In time dinner-services became more elaborate, and many of the items recorded are not used at all today. These included rice saucers, preserve plates, fruit scales and special fish and game services. Chinaware was also designed for serving the new beverages just becoming popular in the 18th century, and chocolate cups, brewing pots (tea-pots) and coffee sets were acquired for this purpose by people living at the Cape.

Advokaat
(One of Mrs Dijkman's recipes, taken from the first Afrikaans cookery book)
'Six wine-glasses brandy, six eggs, two grated nutmegs and white sugar to taste.
Whisk the egg-yolks well and blend in the sugar and nutmeg. Add the brandy and then the stiffly beaten egg-whites and mix everything well. Make three or four hours before required.'
    Advokaat apparently evolved from caudle, a drink similar to the one the Van Riebeecks offered their guests on the birth of their son.

Aniseed brandy
(Another of Mrs Dijkman's recipes from 1890)
'Take a quarter pound of aniseed, two bottles brandy, two pounds of white sugar, bruise the aniseed, steep it in the brandy for 12 days and strain it through a flannel bag. Make a heavy syrup by boiling the sugar and two bottles of water, strain this through the bag as well and stir it into the brandy; shake well and seal tightly.'
(A quarter lb aniseed = 125 g/250 ml
2 lbs white sugar = approximately 1 kg)

Juffertjie-in-'t-groen
200 g (1 cup) white sugar
500 ml (2 cups) brandy
A generous handful of lemon leaves
Measure all ingredients into a saucepan and cover tightly as the saucepan must be airtight.
(In the old days dough was used to seal the saucepan.) Steam for two or three hours over a very low heat until the mixture is well infused. Allow to stand until the next day. Strain, bottle and allow to stand until the sediment has sunk to the bottom and the liqueur is clear.
    Serve in liqueur glasses as a soetsopie.

Orange liqueur
6 bottles of brandy (750 ml each)
3 kg white sugar
Thinly peeled rind of 24 Seville (bitter) oranges and 12 limes
Steep the rind in brandy for three weeks and then strain. Add sugar to brandy. Shake well every day until sugar is dissolved. Decant into bottles and seal with cork and wax.
    Serve in liqueur glasses as a soetsopie.

48 When a baby was baptised, he was often presented with a christening spoon and a silver rattle, and afterwards a toast was drunk to him in advokaat.   **49** A design for the façade of the *Tuynhuys*, residence of the Cape governor. Although this design was never used, the monogram of the Vereenigde Oost-Indische Compagnie marked all its possessions, including the specially commissioned porcelain and glass.

To do full justice to the elegant porcelain dinner-services, cutlery was made from silver. The table fork, which had its origin in Italy, came into general use in Europe at the end of the 17th century and estate inventories indicate that it was adopted at the Cape shortly afterwards. It is mentioned as early as 1705 that a Chinese who had been exiled to the Cape had stolen 24 silver table forks from a widow named Kleijn.

From the estate inventory of Floris Meyboom, and his wife Cornelia de Kock we learn to what extent the Cape burghers used silver tableware. The Meybooms farmed at De Platte Kloof on the slopes of the Tygerberg and on their long family table stood two silver candlesticks, one at either end, the candles casting a soft light over the highly polished silver knives, forks and spoons. In the centre of the table there were silver salt-cellars, a pepper box, sugar castor, oil and vinegar sets, a mustard pot with a spoon and a canister for holding preserve spoons, forks, knives and a pair of tongs, apparently for nuts or loaf sugar. A silver snuffer and snuffer bowl were conveniently at hand for trimming the candles during the meal.

On the governor's table the tableware was even more gracious, and in 1693 an Englishman by the name of Ovington commenting on Governor Simon van der Stel's cutlery, said: '. . . all the Dishes and Plates . . . are made of Massy Silver.'

Cape silversmiths were highly skilled and famous 18th century craftsmen such as Beets, Brewis, Combrinck, Ficker, Heeger, Keet, Lotter, Schmidt and Vos, are remembered for their particularly fine designs. The earliest items manufactured in this country were two communion cups made in 1669 and still preserved in the Groote Kerk in Cape Town. To obtain the silver, craftsman Daniël Egt melted down a hundred silver *rijksdaalders*. Cape silversmiths made many kinds of tableware to order – from full coffee and tea sets, with the chafing dishes for burning coals, to delicate salt spoons. Beautiful silverware has been handed down from these early days and includes marrow spoons with scoops at either end, stew ladles, fish ladles – often with a pierced fish-pattern, soup spoons finely decorated with oak leaves, grape scissors, tea-caddy spoons, pickle forks, chafing dishes and brandy warmers – sometimes with a hinged lid and stinkwood handle. Many of these items fell into disuse, but those that remain reflect the elegance of the table settings of that era.

Goldsmiths fashioned gold tableware, too, although this was not as commonly used as silver. In Simon van der Stel's will we read of two gold dishes, each weighing 1,5 kilograms, as well as two gold cups and saucers.

Copper was used primarily for kitchenware and other household utensils – seldom for tableware. However, a brass coffee pot on a warmer was found in most voorkamers, and copper containers such as sugar canisters and pepper boxes were often used for storage.

The Cape table was also graced with fine glassware and wine was generally served in the beautiful long-stemmed glasses fashionable at the time. These were often decorated with diamond-engraved patterns, the most popular of which featured a bunch of grapes amid vine leaves; decanters were sometimes made to match, as may be seen from a set preserved at Groot Constantia and bearing the VOC monogram.

It was also accepted practice to commemorate important events such as an engagement or baptism with an engraving on glass. Round glasses without stems, called *coupes,* were used for serving a red wine drink to which sugar, lemon juice and eggs were added, and the beverage flavoured with cinnamon. For festive occasions such as wedding banquets, the table was set with large goblets.

Glass for use at the Cape was imported from Holland, Germany or England where the glass-blowers of this period were skilled artists. A considerable quantity was acquired for formal occasions during the years 1781 to 1783 when the French fleet was stationed at Simonstown. There were also coloured glasses, such as the green glass obtained from Germany which was tinted with beech ash, and special glass containers for serving desserts such as seaweed jelly also came into use. Other glassware included salt-cellars, vinegar and oil cruets and water-bottles.

Table-cloths and table napkins were generally made of linen for at that time the Dutch linen industry was highly developed and Flemish weavers excelled in damask work. Before the development of the automatic loom, towards the end of the 18th century, handwoven table-cloths and table napkins from the east and west were used at the Cape and for special occasions, such as a wedding, the napkins were sometimes ingeniously pleated, or even perfumed.

50

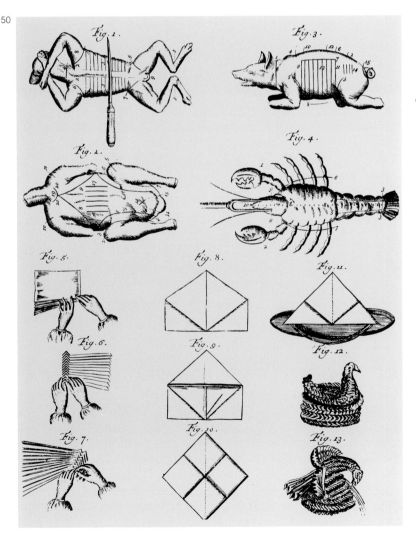

50 A page of diagrams from *De Volmaakte Hollandse Keuken Meid,* a book of household hints published in Holland but used widely at the Cape. Here the reader is shown how to carve a sucking pig, dismember a lobster and fold a table napkin into ornate forms.

With so much beautiful tableware at her disposal the Cape hostess was able to present meals with considerable elegance. We have a fine description from Mary Ann Parker, who touched at the Cape in 1791 while accompanying her husband on a round the world voyage. According to her the tables were beautifully laid, even in the mornings when people sat down to eat fruit. 'Against each person is placed a knife, plate and napkin; thus seated, the Lady of the house makes tea and coffee at a side-table, which the slaves hand round to the company.'

It was general practice for slaves standing behind diners' chairs to drive off flies – a great nuisance at the Cape in those days – with ostrich-feather fans.

THE SERVING OF FOOD

Upon rising in the morning it was the custom in most households to drink tea which was either green or black, the former being the more expensive. Later, tea at this hour was replaced by coffee and rusks. At breakfast at eight o'clock there would be a choice of venison, meat or fish. Wine was usually drunk before the main meal at or about noon when a variety of fish, meat, venison, vegetables and fruit was served. Bowls of fresh fruit – peaches, apricots, grapes, pears and even cantaloup – were usually left on the voorkamer table so that anyone could help himself.

At four o'clock there was coffee or tea with preserves and pastries, while the last meal of the day was served between seven and eight in the evening. At this meal there was the same selection as at midday, and fish, meat, bredie, sosatie, curry or some other meat dish was eaten with fruit and bread.

Sometimes wine was offered as an appetiser before the evening meal although it was mostly drunk at the table. Later in the evening a few glasses of wine or brandied fruits such as *Kaapse jongens* were served. However, well-bred people were expected to drink no more than two or, at most, three glasses of wine.

ENTERTAINING GUESTS

The custom of paying visits was a daily social practice among Capetonians. Guests were gladly welcomed, as were visitors to the Cape, and travellers to the interior enthused about the Afrikaners' hospitality. No appointment was necessary, you were always welcome. There was coffee bubbling constantly on the warmer and the housewife immediately offered her visitor 'the cup that refreshes'. Men were offered a pipe of tobacco, lit from a small smoker's fire-pan brought in by a slave, and often wine was served as well during the visit. In fact, Adam Tas remarked jokingly that he frequently returned from such visits in very high spirits indeed. At dinnertime the guests were invited to share the family meal.

51 The farmer and his family drink coffee made in the kettle standing on its pierced *konfoor* while the itinerant schoolmaster reads from *De Zuid-Afrikaan*. One servant chases off the flies, another clears away the meal and chickens peck at grain spilt from the yellowwood *meelkis*.

81

Johanna Duminy described this as a gracious invitation 'to sit down to a well prepared meal . . . with laughter and conversation'.

The 18th century hostess received her guests in the voorkamer – the room in which the family gathered together and ate. The more elegant houses had a *pronkkamer,* or best room, in which all the family show-pieces were kept; the porcelain cabinet, the silver and the copperware. On anniversaries and Sundays the family would gather here and guests, too, were entertained in this room. The housewife normally sat at a side-table, the *altaartafeltjie,* a foot-stove with glowing coals at her feet. From here she served her guests and saw to it that there were enough coals in the chafing-dishes and foot-warmers. These coals were either raked out from the hearth or else taken from the extinguisher or *doofpot* – the copper pot in which smouldering coals were kept in readiness.

When the weather was fine, families and guests congregated on the stoep that ran along the front of the house. Otto Mentzel describes these warm summer evenings when the entire community sat on their stoeps, exchanged visits, and passed the time in pleasant conversation. The young ladies used the stoep to good effect, and a visiting English wag summed this up when he commented: 'They stoep to conquer.'

People at the Cape often played cards for entertainment when visiting – particularly games such as '*klawerjas*', or '*pam*' and '*l'ombre lanterloo*', a game similar to present-day '*vreetkaart*'. The more seriously inclined played chess, while tric-trac (similar to checkers) and *ganzenbord,* which may be likened to snakes and ladders, were also popular.

Music was another favourite form of entertainment and both ensemble singing and instrumental music were enjoyed. Slave musicians were skilled and well-rehearsed; indeed, it was nothing unusual to see the Malay cook, gardener or coachman exchange his wooden spoon, spade or pair of reins for a clarinet, French

horn or bassoon. The more sumptuous dwellings even had a gallery for the orchestra where slave musicians played during mealtimes, and such a feature may still be seen in Martin Melck's house on the farm Elsenburg near Stellenbosch.

Among the colonists themselves there were musicians, too, and in 1735 Governor de la Fontaine had an organ built and installed for his daughter so that she could entertain his guests.

Dancing was an exceptionally popular pastime and young and old came together to dance away the evening hours. The latest dances were eagerly learned from overseas visitors and, according to Otto Mentzel, the Cape ladies were extremely graceful and lightfooted.

Apart from the general hospitality for which people at the Cape were famous, family gatherings, traditional holidays and other special occasions provided ideal opportunities to organise lavish entertainments.

Koeksisters

240 g cake flour
20 ml (4 teaspoons) baking powder
2 ml (half teaspoon) salt
Fat or oil for frying
25 ml (2 tablespoons) butter
125 ml (half cup) sour milk or buttermilk, or water and lemon juice.

Sift dry ingredients together and rub in butter. Adding the liquid, mix into a soft dough which is easy to knead and knead thoroughly. Leave dough to stand for 15 minutes. Roll out to a thickness of 5 mm and cut into strips 5 mm wide and 70 mm long. Press the ends of two or three strips together and plait. When plaited, press the ends together firmly again.

Deep fry in hot fat or oil until golden brown and well done. Drain and dip into ice cold syrup. Remove, allow excess syrup to drip off and dry on a wire drying rack.

Syrup for koeksisters

1 kg sugar
500 ml (2 cups) water
2 pieces bruised ginger
1 ml (quarter teaspoon) cream of tartar
Pinch of salt
Grated peel and juice of 1 lemon

Measure all the ingredients into a saucepan, heat and stir until the sugar has dissolved and simmer for a few minutes. Remove from heat and chill.

52 The Cape at the beginning of the 19th century epitomised the good life. At all levels it was 'eat, drink and be merry'. **53** 'Didn't I tell you, love, it wouldn't be money misapplied?' Every young lady and gentleman was expected to be familiar with the social graces. **54** Lavish entertainments were the order of the day, even at the Cape.

Milk tart (Melktert)

Flaky pastry is used to line the tart pan. In the old days the dough was made late at night and hung up in a damp muslin cloth in a draught to keep cool. It was baked before sunrise so the cold dough formed light flakes.

Flaky pastry

250 g cake flour
2 ml (half teaspoon) salt
250 g butter
150 ml (half cup) cold water
10 ml (2 teaspoons) brandy

Use ice water and have all the other ingredients very cold. Work in a cold place. Make sure that the dough does not stick to the table or rolling pin. Tart pans are never greased.

Sift the cake flour and salt together. Rub a fifth of the butter into the flour. Using a knife, mix in the water and brandy to form a stiff dough. Knead the dough until it feels waxy and elastic (approximately three minutes).

Divide the remaining butter into three portions. Hard butter should be grated. Roll out the dough very thinly and place one portion of the butter on the dough in small pieces. Sprinkle with a little flour. Fold over the dough, roll out and seal at the edges. Allow to stand in a cool place for 10 minutes. Repeat procedure with remaining two portions of butter. Roll out thinly and place dough in tart pan. Lay strips of dough around the edge of the pan to form a ridge, using beaten egg-yolk to stick strips down. Bake in a very hot oven (230° C).

Filling

35 g (2 tablespoons) cake flour
60 g (4 tablespoons) sugar
500 ml (2 cups) milk
2 eggs
5 ml (1 teaspoon) grated orange peel
Pinch of salt

Combine the dry ingredients and make into a paste with a little milk. Bring the rest of the milk to the boil, add the flour mixture and boil for three minutes. Allow to cool slightly. Add beaten egg-yolks. Fold in whisked egg-whites and grated orange peel. Pour while still hot into a tart dish lined with raw flaky pastry. Bake in a hot oven (200° C) for 10 minutes, reduce the temperature to 190° C and bake for another 10 minutes. Sprinkle with cinnamon-sugar when it comes out of the oven.

THE WEDDING RECEPTION

Of all the family celebrations, none was more splendid than the wedding reception. The Cape was renowned for its pretty young brides, for a great many officials who called here found their life's companions. In numerous old writings there are glowing references to the charm of the local young women, and Mentzel wrote that they were very pretty, more so than girls in other parts of the world since their complexions were unblemished by pockmarks.

He described their dress as simple yet elegant, without extravagance, and their headdresses, he wrote, consisted of neat bonnets of the kind worn in France, rather than the high pointed variety which he referred to as 'the tower of Babel'. Everyday dresses, made from fine East Indian calico (cotton), had starched collars and aprons. Dresses made of silk were worn only on holidays, to wedding receptions and at other festivities when the women were very elegantly dressed without being ostentatious.

Courtship between a young girl and an amorous swain gave rise to the Afrikaner custom of the *opsitkers,* or courting candle, from which a young man could deduce how well-disposed the young woman was towards him. The length of the candle in the voorkamer indicated how long he was welcome to call on her.

After the courtship he would propose marriage and if the girl accepted, her parents were asked to give their consent and a 'promise of marriage' was made. The young couple then announced publicly that they were to marry, and with this the festivities began. Friends and family visited the parents of the bride to congratulate the happy couple and these guests were

55

offered something to drink and a selection of pastries. The engagement was short and the wedding normally took place on the third Sunday afternoon after the marriage announcement.

On the night of the marriage a wedding dinner for invited guests – for the most part relations and friends – was held at the bride's

55 Where fashions were concerned the Cape was only as far behind Europe as the time it took a sailing ship to cross the ocean. **56** An engagement tea. The *pièce de résistance* here is melktert but the table is also spread with syrup-drenched koeksisters, raisin tart, sponge cake, toasted almonds, soetkoekies, preserved figs and jam tarts.

parents' house. During this celebration the bridal couple sat in the voorkamer, beneath a large mirror decorated with a heart-shaped garland of flowers and ribbons. Guests were received by the *speelnote* – that is, the bridesmaid and best man – and introduced to the bridal couple, the bridesmaid customarily introducing the guests to the bridegroom while the best man introduced them to the bride. The festivities began in earnest with the filling of a large glass goblet – the so-called 'love cup' – to the brim with choice wine and this was passed among all those present. Everyone took a long sip from it in honour of the newlyweds and after that toasts –

Wedding Menu

Fruit cocktail with brandied grapes

Crayfish cocktail

Roast sucking pig with orange

Chicken pie   Mutton tamarind

Yellow rice with raisins

Stuffed spring pumpkin

Fresh garden peas

Quince sambal

Water-cress salad

Pancakes with Van der Hum

Coffee

Wine jelly
25 ml (2 tablespoons) gelatine
50 ml (4 tablespoons) cold water
300 ml (1,25 cups) boiling water
10 cloves
2 ml (half teaspoon) citric acid
75 ml (6 tablespoons) sugar
250 ml (1 cup) sweet wine
2 sticks cinnamon
5 ml (1 teaspoon) lemon essence

Add boiling water to sugar, cloves and stick cinnamon and simmer for 10 minutes. Soak gelatine in the cold water and then dissolve it in mixture and allow to cool. Add citric acid, lemon essence and wine and allow to set. Serve in jelly glasses.

In the old days either isinglass or seaweed jelly was used instead of gelatine. The seaweed was sun-dried and all the sand was removed. It was then washed thoroughly, wrapped in a muslin cloth and boiled in water, strained and used as a base for jellied desserts.

which were sometimes very long and jovial – were drunk to their health.

Then the food was served, all the dishes being brought to the table simultaneously according to custom. At the traditional wedding dinner the main dishes were usually served whole; for instance roasted sucking pigs with oranges in their mouths were placed at either end of the table where they could make a fine display. This was followed by other traditional Cape dishes and Lady Anne Barnard describes such a wedding feast at which the following were served: Cape ham, turkeys, ducks, chickens, geese, venison, partridges, mutton, fish, vegetables, stewed beans, cabbage, egg pudding, tartlets and various

57 Wine jelly, served from an Imariware bowl, sparkles in stemmed Dutch glasses and Cape silver gleams on the slate-topped table. A species of seaweed – *Suhria vittata* – was often boiled to provide a nourishing base for jellied desserts.

other pastries, fruit and strawberries. Otto Mentzel also describes an instance when no fewer than 52 different kinds of food were placed on the table.

Guests did not sit around the table but on chairs arranged along the walls, and while etiquette demanded that the men serve the ladies, if the ladies wanted second helpings they had to fetch them themselves. Slaves served coffee, tea, chocolate, almond milk, wine and beer to the guests.

It was not unusual for the Governor to make his orchestra available for such a wedding feast and after the meal the tables were removed and the guests then danced until midnight. Some of the older people who did not dance would play cards or 'kept themselves busy with good conversation and a glass of wine' until it was time to go home.

THE CHRISTENING FEAST

One of the first celebrations recorded at the Cape was the christening feast given by the Van Riebeecks on the birth of their son. One gathers that at that time it was customary to offer the guests at the feast a large bowl of caudle, and the Van Riebeecks ordered eggs for this warm spiced drink. Instead of a spoon for stirring the drink, a stick of cinnamon with a ribbon tied to it was used and the length of the stick and the colour of the ribbon indicated the infant's sex. The proud father served the caudle himself and the merry-making is described in an old ditty which went approximately like this:

Proud new father,
stir the caudle
Slice the cake
and hand it round
Cake and caudle,
both are noble
With long life
may they all be crowned.

THE FUNERAL RECEPTION

A funeral was a major social occasion at the Cape, so much so that over the years it was continually necessary to promulgate laws to make the proceedings less extravagant. Funerals were sometimes

Almond milk

This drink was usually served at wedding receptions and according to an old recipe it was prepared as follows:

'Quarter pound peeled, sweet almonds are finely ground, steeped in a can of water for one hour, rubbed through a muslin cloth and sugar added according to taste.'

Burnt almonds

300 g (2 cups) almonds, shelled but not blanched
400 g (2 cups) sugar
5 ml (1 teaspoon) dried naartje peel, pounded and sifted
2 ml (half teaspoon) ground ginger
2,5 ml (half teaspoon) cake flour
12,5 ml (1 tablespoon) red bolus (ferri-oxide mixture)

Mix sugar, spices and red bolus. Add half a cup (125 ml) water, bring to the boil slowly, stirring to dissolve the sugar, and boil for about 5 minutes. Add almonds and flour mixed with a little water and stir well. Boil without stirring until mixture is thick. Pour into a pan greased with butter and break into pieces before it cools.

Almond tart

Flaky pastry
250 g pounded almonds
250 g sugar
3 eggs, separated
90 g (6 tablespoons) cake flour
A little finely shredded orange/naartje peel
12,5 ml (1 tablespoon) lemon juice
12,5 ml (1 tablespoon) butter

Stir the sugar and beaten egg-yolks together. Beat butter well and stir in all the other ingredients. Mix well. Beat egg-whites and fold into the mixture. Line a tart pan with flaky pastry, pour in the filling and bake in a hot oven (200° C) for 20 minutes.

Yellow rice with raisins

Funerals, as well as auctions, were usually followed by big meals to cater for those who had to travel long distances by ox-wagon or horse-carriage. Yellow rice with raisins was so much a part of these meals that it became known as 'funeral rice' or 'auction rice'.

750 ml (3 cups) boiling water
200 g (1 cup) rice
1 stick cinnamon
2 ml (half teaspoon) turmeric
5 ml (1 teaspoon) salt
50 ml (4 tablespoons) yellow sugar
12,5 ml (1 tablespoon) butter
90 g seedless raisins

Add all ingredients except raisins to boiling water and allow to cook slowly until almost done. Stir in raisins lightly and allow to steam over low heat.

held in the evening and for these about 20 lantern-bearers were hired to light the way for the cortège. Similarly, special *huilebalke*, or weepers, who mourned aloud, and *trop sluiters* or procession joiners, who brought up the rear of the procession to make it longer, could be hired. Wooden hatchments displaying the family crests of the dead can still be seen on the walls of the Groote Kerk in Cape Town.

After the funeral everyone who had been to the cemetery, including the hired participants and onlookers who had joined the procession out of curiosity, was treated to a meal at the home of the deceased. Old estate accounts record the food served at such a funeral feast and make mention of hams, geese, turkeys, chickens, ducks, raisins, almonds, cake, bread, cheese, as well as liquor and tobacco. At the funeral of Joachim von Dessin a barrel of beer and 40 bottles of red wine were consumed. Adam Tas sent five pails of wine, a Cape ham, three legs of mutton and bread to the funeral of a servant who had drowned. In some writings reference is made to *geraspte* or *chraspe* loaves being served at funeral feasts. These were possibly a kind of cake which looked like bread, although some historians think that it was white bread with a crisp texture – hence the word *chraspe*. Other dishes, too, were regular fare at funerals and this is the origin of the name 'funeral rice' for yellow rice with raisins.

58 Funerals were important events in 18th century Cape Town as can be seen from this impressive cortège accompanying the coffin of Baron von Rheede van Oudtshoorn in 1773. Mourners often travelled great distances on these occasions and were invited afterwards to share in the lavish funeral feast.

BIRTHDAY CELEBRATIONS

Birthdays were gay affairs, especially when the father, as head of the family, celebrated his anniversary. On this occasion many friends would come to the house to congratulate him. The best table-cloth was used and milk tarts, coconut, raisin and almond tarts and other pastries such as patty-cakes, or *kolwyntjies*, koeksisters and tartlets were served. With the tea and coffee, wine jelly in small glasses and preserves, such as citron and watermelon, were offered as well.

The birthdays of other members of the family were festive as well. The chair of the person whose birthday it was would be decorated with flowers, and young ladies sometimes received poems from admirers. One such token of affection was dedicated to 'the virtuous and lovely maiden Grisella Mostaart, when her birthday arrives on 19th September, *anno* 1673 at the Cape of Good Hope.' It reads as follows:

'Pick myrtle, thyme and Virgin Palm
Pluck harp-string, sing a joyful psalm
Filled with resounding Melody,
Celebrate in a season so lovely
The anniversary of one endowed so well
As may in highest Heaven dwell
Grisella Mostaarts, dearest wight
In whom be comfort and all delight
A virgin blessed with virtue and grace
Perfect of soul, of limb, of face
The idol of every girl and boy
The young man's very hope and joy.'

NEW YEAR'S DAY

This was considered to be the most important day of the year, and the New Year was ushered in at daybreak with a salvo of cannon-fire from the walls of the Castle. Ships in the bay were decked out with flags and bunting and the officers and other members of the

Political Council paid a formal visit to the Governor between eight and nine o'clock in the morning to convey their good wishes and enjoy the choice confections and music.

All Capetonians spent New Year's day in cheerful celebration, and picnics on Table Mountain were a regular feature. The hamper on such occasions contained all kinds of delicacies and Mentzel describes one from which cooked ham, cold leg of mutton, cold beef, bread rolls and butter as well as a flask of East Indian arrack were unpacked when the picnickers reached the top of Table Mountain.

60

CHRISTMAS

Christmas was primarily a religious holiday, but special delicacies were prepared: sweet cookies, macaroons and tartlets, or turnovers, were ready in the pantry and cold ginger beer, brewed in earthenware pitchers, brought relief from the heat. Chicken pie and sucking pig, duck and other roast poultry – particularly turkey – over the years became the traditional Christmas fare. Later in the afternoon large watermelons were cut up and the long slices broken away from the crown. The slices were usually given to the children who played pranks, washing one another's faces with the rinds, while the delectable crown was enjoyed by the adults.

Chicken pie
1 chicken
Mace leaves
6 whole pimentos
12 peppercorns
3 cloves
2 onions
30 g (2 tablespoons) sago
1 wine-glass of wine
1 egg-yolk
Juice of 1 lemon
Hardboiled egg, sliced
Flaky pastry
Cook the chicken with the herbs, spices and onion until tender and remove bones from cooked meat. Soak the sago until soft, stir the sago into the boned meat and simmer. As soon as the sago is translucent, add white wine, beaten egg and lemon juice. Stir until thick and creamy and then spoon into a pie dish lined with pastry and cover with slices of hard-boiled egg. Cover with pastry and bake in a hot oven (200° C) for 15 to 20 minutes.

Game pie
Prepare meat as for stewed venison (p. 26). Remove the large bones and excess liquid. Put into a pie dish and cover with slices of hard-boiled egg. Cover with pie crust, scallop the edge, coat with beaten egg-yolk and bake in a hot oven (200°C).

59 From the earliest days of the settlement – as recorded by Jan van Riebeeck himself – picnics were a popular form of entertainment, particularly to celebrate the new year. Here Huguenot immigrants enjoy a meal in the open while a Hottentot servant waits on them. **60** New Year 1741 – and Pieter van Laar, like many other children at the Cape, went to infinite pains inscribing and decorating a greetings card for his parents.

Braaivleis

A cheerful meal around a braaivleis fire is a South African custom. All kinds of meat cuts are grilled over the coals, but ribs of mutton remain the favourite, served as follows:

Ribs of mutton

Chop the ribs into pieces the right size for serving. Sprinkle with salt and pepper, grill over glowing coals, spread with butter and serve hot.

Corned ribs of mutton

Ribs of mutton
125 g (half cup) salt
12,5 ml (1 teaspoon) sugar
2 ml (half teaspoon) saltpetre

Mix salt, sugar and saltpetre and rub into the ribs. Leave to stand for two days, turning frequently. Then hang up to allow to drain and to dry in the wind. Boil until tender and grill over hot coals.

FAIRS

Old documents make occasional mention of fairs at which the merry-makers apparently sometimes ran riot. Indeed some of the commanders at the Cape were reprimanded by the Lords Seventeen for permitting these functions to get out of hand.

The most famous fair, the one celebrating Simon van der Stel's birthday, was held between 1 and 14 October each year when the burghers streamed to Stellenbosch to take part in the fun. The climax of the fair was the target-shooting competition on 14th October. The participants fired at a wooden parrot set on top of a pole, and were allowed to do so from any position outside a radius of 35 metres from the target. Every competitor who shot a wing or the head of the target received a prize and to shatter the entire bird was considered a great achievement and entitled the marksman, in addition to a cash prize, to claim the title of 'King of the Marksmen' for the entire year. After the competition everyone drank a toast to Governor van der Stel's health before returning home. It is believed that the Afrikaans words *kermisbed* (shakedown) and *vleisbraai* (barbecue) originated at these fairs, for during the festivities an ox or sheep was usually spit-roasted.

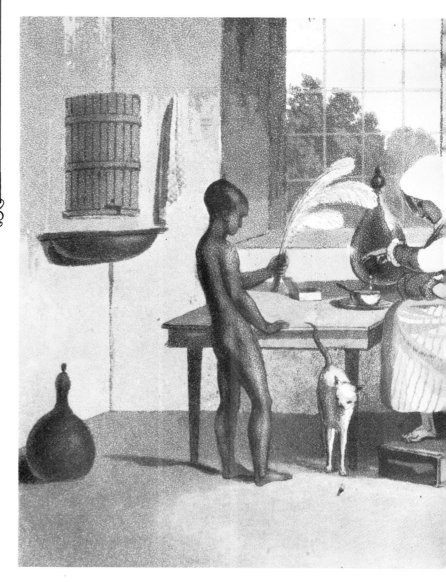

AUCTIONS

Among the farming communities these gatherings usually took the form of fairs at which cattle, poultry and other livestock were offered for sale as well as items such as home produce. Food and drink or even a meal was served, and everyone made the most of this opportunity to come together and enjoy one another's company. In her diary Johanna Duminy claims that the burghers enjoyed themselves at these country events, and elsewhere it is recorded that slaves served those present with cakes, tarts and other pastries and that tea, wine and beer – as well as glowing coals with which to light pipes – were provided. Apparently it was hoped that such hospitality would encourage the buyers to spend more.

HARVEST FESTIVALS

Until very recently in the Boland harvest festivals were held on farms after the last sheaf of grain had been stacked on the rick or the last of the grapes harvested. According to custom, lemonade, or *wijnschotel* – a punch prepared from wine, orange leaves and

Lemon punch or Wijnschotel

A few slices of toasted white bread
A few bottles of wine
Nutmeg
Lemon leaves

Cut the toast into cubes, sprinkle with grated nutmeg and place in a basin containing the wine and the lemon juice.

Lemon punch was served to the workers on farms during the festival held to celebrate the end of the harvesting. It was also served to guests. The mother of the well-known Johanna Duminy offered it to her guests when they returned from a climb on Table Mountain.

61 A country housewife surrounded by her simple possessions. In remote areas families depended for their meat largely upon wild game shot in the veld. On returning home the farmer would wash his hands in water drawn from the corner barrel into the basin beneath and dry them on the towel. Then he would hang his powder horn, his overcoat and his wide-awake hat on the wall.

Pot-roasted Joints

To pot-roast meat in the old Cape style, use a heavy-bottomed saucepan. Prepare the joint and place it in a saucepan on the stove with approximately 1 cup (250 ml) water. Cover the saucepan and allow the meat to cook slowly.

Add small quantities of water until the meat changes colour and then add salt and fat. Turn and baste constantly with the meat stock until the meat is browned. When the meat is almost done, add a little red wine mixed with flour to thicken the gravy. Instead of water, wine may be added while the meat is roasting.

Pot-roasted leg of mutton

Wipe clean a leg of mutton. Slice through evenly to the bone and insert chopped parsley, salt, pepper, finely chopped onion, grated nutmeg, a mace leaf and a few cloves between the slices. Skewer slices together, pour a large glass of wine over the joint and pot-roast in the Cape manner.

Pot-roasted chicken, duck or muscovy duck

Prepare the bird, twist legs up against the carcase and secure with a skewer. Cut the wings in the first joint and twist along back. Sprinkle with flour and a glass of white wine and pot-roast in the Cape manner.

Poultry was sometimes served with a stuffing. Favourite stuffings were:

Bread stuffing

1 finely chopped onion
Half a nutmeg, grated
1 lump of butter about the size of an egg
5 ml (1 teaspoon) finely ground thyme
60 g (half cup) fresh breadcrumbs
Salt and pepper
Mix all the ingredients well and fill the cleaned stomach cavity of the bird with the stuffing. Fold the legs along the stomach and secure with a skewer.

Meat stuffing

Make small, savoury meatballs and stuff the bird in the way described for bread stuffing.

Bread dumplings (served with poultry)

Soak three slices of day-old white bread in poultry stock until soft. Squeeze out excess moisture, place in a saucepan and stir in a knob of butter, salt, pepper and grated nutmeg. Add two beaten eggs and stir well. Make into small round balls and roll in flour. Bring to the boil in poultry stock. Pour off the stock and serve the dumplings with the poultry.

62 Among sophisticated Cape landowners, duckshooting was a favourite sport. The small *balie* holds salt for dressing the bird.

cinnamon, to which cubes of toast were added just before serving – was provided. It was served from an earthenware basin with a large ladle into the drinking mugs of the thirsty workers, bringing the year's harvesting to a merry close.

THE GOVERNOR'S RECEPTIONS

These functions varied from jolly carouses for the mariners to very formal and sedate affairs.

Van Riebeeck describes how he entertained the officers of an English ship so that eventually 'they went on board dancing, leaping about and rolling from side to side, in high spirits and well-contented'.

The beautiful reception halls at Groot Constantia, Vergelegen and the Castle testify to the grace and elegance of these splendid receptions at which the colourfully dressed guests usually arrived in coaches. According to Lady Anne Barnard, hostess at the Castle, these glittering occasions formed an integral part of the way of life at the Cape.

The governors gave smaller, more intimate dinners as well. The clergyman Valentyn described how one night, as the guest of Governor Willem Adriaan van der Stel on the farm Vergelegen, he partook with relish of the excellent fish dishes – including steenbras – and the delicious fruit and superb wines set before him.

Governor Simon van der Stel was also fond of entertaining guests at his magnificent farm Constantia. Here the renowned Constantia wines, made by the Governor himself who was something of a wine connoisseur, accompanied the delectable Cape fare of fish, roast venison, eland pie and fresh local fruit which he ordered set before his guests. Old writings make regular reference to the fact that the Governor's table was always beautifully appointed – a feast for the eye as well as the palate.

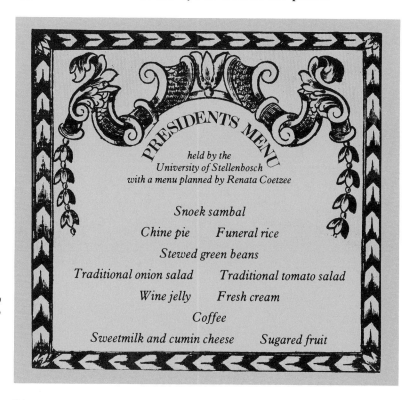

PRESIDENTS MENU

held by the
University of Stellenbosch
with a menu planned by Renata Coetzee

Snoek sambal

Chine pie   Funeral rice

Stewed green beans

Traditional onion salad   Traditional tomato salad

Wine jelly   Fresh cream

Coffee

Sweetmilk and cumin cheese   Sugared fruit

Perlemoen (abalone)

Remove abalone from shell and wash well to remove all sand and mucus. Beat with a mallet until soft and wash again. Mince and add half as much again of fine, white breadcrumbs, and simmer slowly in butter in a heavy-bottomed saucepan until tender – about half an hour. Stir in more butter, grated nutmeg and white pepper. Sprinkle with salt just before serving. Serve on rice and sprinkle with cayenne pepper.

Perdevoetjies (periwinkles)

Boil the perdevoetjies for 20 minutes in sea-water. Break open the shells and eat the soft inner flesh.

Periwinkles

Cook in shells for approximately 20 minutes. Remove the meat. Do not use the flat disc on the one side or the intestines at the back. Wash off all the sand, mince and prepare in the same way as abalone.

Stewed white mussels

Wash the mussels and steam in boiling water until the shells open – about ten minutes. Remove from shells and clean. Simmer the mussels until tender in milk flavoured with a little nutmeg, salt and pepper. Then thicken with flour and stir in a little cream and a wine-glass of white wine.

Stewed oysters

Wash the oysters and boil for a few minutes. Remove from shells, clean and simmer until tender in butter to which a chopped onion, a teaspoon of parsley, breadcrumbs, capers and lemon juice have been added.

63 Here, served on blue and white oriental porcelain with white wine to wash the meal down, are lobster, perlemoen and mussels. It was the *Strandlopers* – primitive beach-combers of Van Riebeeck's day – who introduced the first settlers to a variety of local shellfish, which later the skills of the Cape housewife transformed into dishes fit for an epicure.

OTHER SOCIAL FUNCTIONS

A visiting fleet was not only an important social event at the Cape, but also the only way in which local people could acquire various commodities and hear news from abroad. It was therefore an occasion greeted with great excitement, and many Capetonians gathered on the wharf to invite the visitors to their homes. Although the guests were expected to pay for their accommodation, this hospitality was eagerly received by travellers faced with the hazards of the second arduous stage of their journey around the southern tip of Africa. Some sailors made the most of this

Dried fruit (as dessert)
Soak dried fruit overnight and steam with a little sugar, naartje peel and a small glass of sherry. Serve cold with thin cream.

Baked apples or quinces
Wash well and core. Make a few small incisions on the sides and insert cloves. Pour honey over the top and bake until soft in a slow oven (140° C). Serve with thin cream.

break in the long sea journey and spent their money lavishly thereby acquiring the name 'lords for six weeks'. They frequently sold, exchanged or bartered goods with their hosts, items that were subsequently sold to other Capetonians at a great profit. This custom led to the coining of the apt saying among the locals: 'Our livelihood is from God and from Strangers.'

On the first Sunday after the fleet's departure all excess commodities purchased were put on display in the voorkamers of the Cape homes and offered for sale. In the 18th century there were as yet no shops at the Cape, and only local produce such as fruit and ostrich feathers could be sold on the market square. Most sought after items offered for sale in the voorkamers were spices, dinner services, porcelain vases and brightly coloured Eastern fabrics. Foodstuffs such as cumin cheese and sweetmilk cheese, barrels of salt pork, ham, tongue, pickled herrings and salmon from the ships' stores also found their way surreptitiously into the voorkamers. Although the sailors grew tired of this fare, it was snapped up by the Capetonians who welcomed a change of diet and it was frequently served at such special occasions as wedding receptions.

CHURCH ATTENDANCE

From the very outset the Church played an important role in the spiritual and social life of the people at the Cape.

During the first 13 years religious services were held in the fort. Later, while the Castle was under construction, a wooden shed was adapted for the purpose. However, after the Castle had been completed, services were held there. It was only in 1700 that the cornerstone of the Groote Kerk was laid by Willem Adriaan van der Stel and the church building came into use for the first time in 1704.

64 A copper tart pan makes the ideal receptacle for apples baked with honey and served with cream. Quinces are equally delicious when prepared in the same way.
65 Table Bay at the end of the 18th century. The arrival of passing ships was a signal for celebration and weary mariners welcomed the delicious food and wine and hospitable entertainment pressed on them by their hosts.

66 Greenmarket Square was the place where the Cape Town housewife obtained her fresh vegetables and where horses, cattle and wagons were bought and sold. *Toerings* and top hats, *doeks* and stylish bonnets were to be seen everywhere and it was here that people of every walk of life assembled to hear important announcements made from the stoep of the old Town House.

101

Tartlets

*Roll out flaky pastry to a thickness of
approximately 5 mm. Cut out rounds of dough
with a glass, place a dab of smooth apricot jam
in the middle of each round of dough, fold in
half, coat the edges with a little beaten egg-yolk
and press together firmly. Brush with beaten
egg-yolk and bake in a very hot oven (200° –
220° C) for about 10 minutes.*

Crackling cake

1 kg cake flour
750 g brown sugar
25 ml (2 tablespoons) ground cinnamon
25 ml (2 tablespoons) ground ginger
6 ml (1 large teaspoon) bicarbonate of soda
6 ml (1 large teaspoon) cream of tartar
500 ml (2 cups) pounded crackling
*Enough hot buttermilk or clabbered milk (curds
and whey) to make a stiff dough.*

*Mix the dry ingredients, add the crackling and
mix into a stiff dough with the hot milk. Roll
out thickly and cut into small oblongs. Bake in
flat pans in a hot oven (200° C) for about 20
minutes.*

Commander van Riebeeck laid great stress on church attendance and decreed that 'no one may absent themselves, whatever their feelings may be, without consent, on pain of punishment'. If a man failed once to attend, he forfeited his wine ration, a month's wages were forfeited the second time and the third offence was punishable by a year's hard labour in chains without pay.

After Sunday morning service the Commander allowed everyone – because all had to work hard during the week – to rest for the remainder of the day. Van Riebeeck himself was fond of going fishing on Sunday afternoons or visiting the free burghers on their little farms.

After Van Riebeeck's time, when the Groote Kerk was used for religious services, the men sat on benches, while the women sat on chairs so that there was sufficient room for their wide dresses. The Governor and his sons sat a special pew to the right of the pulpit and his wife and daughters took their places on chairs that had been set on the carpet that led from his pew to the outside of the church. When the Governor entered the church everyone had to rise. Directly opposite him sat the Political Council, military officers and other officials according to rank. Two rows of benches were placed along the side-walls for important visitors, while the ordinary burghers occupied the back rows.

Chairs for the women were placed in the centre of the church and they were all seated according to social status. In later years they were carried in sedan chairs to the front of the pulpit while slaves brought in their Bibles, cushions and foot-warmers.

67 Good food must take its toll. The young women of the Cape were renowned for their slim figures and good looks – but the matrons clearly enjoyed their own cooking more than was good for them! **68** Sophistication and extravagance soon earned for Cape Town its nickname of 'Little Paris'. Here vegetable hawkers, a water-carrier and a slave in disgrace look on as liveried servants carry a sedan chair across Greenmarket Square.

The competition between women for social status in the church is delightfully depicted in the following verse:

*Maggie found that a woman
had taken her chair
And said she would very soon
chase her from there.
Such a fuss, said the other,
about nothing, my dear,
You sit here every week
and I once a year.*

This rivalry reached its peak during Governor Ryk Tulbagh's term of office (1751 – 1771). In his efforts to keep the burghers, particularly the women, in check he issued his 'pomp and circumstance' laws which decreed that women were no longer permitted to enter the church in sedan chairs and had to carry their own Bibles. If their dress was too extravagant – for example if they sported a train – the women were fined. They were no longer allowed to walk beneath umbrellas borne by special pages – only one of the many excessive displays that led to the Cape's earning the nickname 'Little Paris'.

But, although pomp and ceremony sometimes got out of hand, sober good taste and gracious living were nevertheless more in character for the majority of the people at the Cape during the 17th and 18th centuries.

68

OTHER SOCIAL CUSTOMS

In addition to the specific social events already mentioned, the local people sometimes took strolls in what were originally the Company's Gardens or went on journeys or hunting expeditions. There were a few individuals, such as Henning Huising on his farm Meerlust, who took part in target-shooting competitions or

Ginger nuts
1 kg sifted flour
500 g butter
30 g (2 tablespoons) bicarbonate of soda
60 ml (quarter cup) milk
200 g (1 cup) sugar
37,5 ml (3 tablespoons) ground ginger
1 egg
1 kg moskonfyt (or honey or syrup)
Rub the butter into the flour. Mix bicarbonate of soda with milk. Add all the other ingredients and make into a dough with moskonfyt, honey or syrup. Leave to stand overnight. Knead thoroughly the next morning. Shape into round balls the size of a large marble, make a dent in the middle of each ginger nut and bake in a medium oven (180° C) for 10 to 15 minutes.

Aniseed cookies
110 g (half cup) butter
110 g (half cup) fat
500 g (2 cups) sugar
250 ml (1 cup) milk
5 ml (1 teaspoon) cream of tartar
10 g (1 tablespoon) bicarbonate of soda
225 g (1 small cup) aniseed
1,5 kg cake flour
Melt the butter and fat and stir in sugar and milk. Add bicarbonate of soda. Rub cream of tartar into the flour. Stir aniseed and flour into the milk mixture. Knead well, roll out and cut into rounds with a glass. Bake in a medium oven (180° C) for 10 to 15 minutes.

Macaroons
500 g almonds, peeled and pounded
400 g castor sugar
5 egg-whites
Warm sugar slightly, mix in almonds and lightly fold in stiffly beaten egg-whites. Line a baking pan with paper and grease with butter. Spoon mounds of egg-white mixture onto the paper. Bake for 25 minutes in a slow oven (140° C).

Sorrel sauce

Half cup sorrel, finely chopped
120 g (1 cup) breadcrumbs
Knob of butter
Pinch of salt
Boil the sorrel, stir in the salt, butter and breadcrumbs and boil together for a few minutes.
  Serve with fish, poultry or curry.

Mince sauce

50 ml (4 tablespoons) chopped mint
25 ml (2 tablespoons) castor sugar
A small glassful of wine
Place the chopped mint leaves in a saucepan and stir in the sugar and wine. Heat and stir until the sugar has melted. Prepare the sauce three hours before the meal to allow the wine to draw.
  Serve with fish, game, mutton or other meat.

Salad dressing (Mayonnaise)

4 hard-boiled eggs
5 ml (1 teaspoon) prepared mustard
Pinch of salt
50 ml (4 tablespoons) cream
Vinegar
Pinch of chilli powder.
Mash the egg-yolks and add the other ingredients. Mix thoroughly and add vinegar.

Sauce for game

30 g (2 tablespoons) currants
250 ml (1 cup) water
120 g (1 cup) breadcrumbs
6 cloves
1 wine-glass port
Knob of butter
Boil currants in the water for a few minutes. Add the other ingredients and stir until the mixture is smooth.

Herb vinegar

1,5 l good quality vinegar
12,5 ml (1 tablespoon) mustard seed
12,5 ml (1 tablespoon) whole pimentos
12,5 ml (1 tablespoon) whole cloves
A few sticks of cinnamon
Tie herbs into muslin bag, place in vinegar and allow to stand for one month. Shake the vinegar occasionally. Use over salad or in the preparation of meat and fish.

Chilli vinegar

Boil a few small onions and a few pieces of ginger in vinegar. Strain and allow to cool. Take a green and a red chilli, prick with a needle, sprinkle with salt and place in jar. Pour cold vinegar over the chilli. Seal.

organised cock fights on their farms, and in 1708 a bull-baiting match was held at the Castle. These were largely the exceptions, however, and life was generally quiet, peaceful and family orientated.

The wife was the focal point of the family and she busied herself all day long with her domestic chores. After early morning tea and breakfast, she assigned to the slaves their various daily tasks; some had to irrigate the vegetable gardens, others had to bake bread, operate the churn or prepare the midday meal. The silver and copperware had to be polished, too, and the washing sorted and allocated.

After the midday meal everyone retired to rest, but by four o'clock the kitchen was once more the hub of activity; tea was made and guests received, or friends visited. As evening approached the poultry had to be fed and the eggs collected.

When the time came to light the candles and lamps, some adults preferred to play cards for a while and had their supper only after the children had been put to bed. On the other hand, some families made the evening meal a time when all the members of the family came together, in which case entertainment commenced only after the family meal and devotions.

In the 17th and 18th centuries women played a vital role in the social life at the Cape. Their cookery in particular was highly praised, as this contemporary homily illustrates:
  'Health, cheerfulness and a good humour
  all depend, in truth, on a good kitchen.'

CHAPTER SIX
THE FIRST COOKERY BOOKS

The young ladies at the Cape received formal instruction in reading, writing, arithmetic and music. According to Mrs Kindersley, who visited the Cape and published a book in 1777, they were all capable of speaking, in addition to Dutch, fairly good English and French – which they learnt from visitors. Portuguese they picked up from the slaves. But above all, they were taught how to run a home and to cook; indeed no young girl was considered ready for marriage until she could bake bread and prepare a good meal. Mothers were responsible for training their daughters to prepare meat. For this purpose the old Dutch cookery books were no longer of any use and many women therefore compiled their own. Such handwritten records are in fact the first South African cookery books and, fortunately, some of these valuable documents have been preserved in museums, in libraries and in private collections.

70

The oldest cookery book written in South Africa was the *Mondprovisie Boekje* of Johanna van Riebeeck, granddaughter of Jan van Riebeeck, who compiled it during her visit to the Cape in 1710. These recipes were intended specifically for the preparation of food suitable for long sea journeys. Thus she includes a recipe for dried bread in which a pound of unsifted flour, yeast, a spoonful of butter and water are made into a thin batter. The well-beaten mixture is left to stand for a while to rise, and afterwards baked and dried. Dishes such as this are for the most part completely foreign to the later development of traditional South African cookery – with the exception of a recipe for pickled snoek prepared by the wife of a Cape *heemraad* for the ocean journey.

Braised meat
Use diced meat or poultry. Braise the meat and shredded onion until brown in a heavy-bottomed saucepan. Add water, cover and simmer gently until tender. To make gravy, thicken the stock in which the meat was cooked and add flavouring to taste.
  Serve with rice.

Chine, mutton or lamb pie
2 kg mutton chine or leg of mutton
2 onions, chopped
250 ml (1 cup) dry white wine
250 ml (1 cup) vinegar
5 ml (1 teaspoon) basil
2 ml (half teaspoon) ground cloves
20 g (4 teaspoons) salt
500 ml (2 cups) meat stock
Flaky pastry

Chop meat into pieces. Sauté onions and meat in butter or oil in a heavy-bottomed saucepan. Add all the ingredients and simmer until done. Remove the bones and drain excess liquid before spooning the meat into a pie dish. Place some bones on top of the meat to support the crust, cover with pie crust and bake for about 20 minutes in a hot oven (200° C).

69 This farmer's family keeps the Sabbath with time-honoured solemnity. Rifle and hunting hat are idle, coffee cups empty, and father in his shirt sleeves reads from the family Bible. **70** Even girls from the humblest homes were expected to be adequate cooks before they were ready for marriage.

Desserts

Baked and steamed desserts such as vinegar pudding and duff began to appear on the table after the arrival of the British settlers in the 19th century. Before that, lighter desserts such as rice with cinnamon and sugar (rijstebrij) and fresh fruit were served to round off a meal.

Blancmange with peach leaves

(Derived from blanc-manger *which, in the 15th century, was made from almond milk)*

1,5 l milk
60 g gelatine
125 g sugar
4 peach leaves (for almond flavour)
Rind of 1 lemon

Dissolve gelatine in a little cold water and stir in the warm milk. Add the other ingredients and heat to boiling point. Then simmer gently for 10 minutes, stirring all the time. Remove leaves and rind and pour into a wetted jelly mould. Turn out when set and decorate with apricot jam or with flowers.

Pumpkin fritters *(as dessert)*

500 ml (2 cups) cooked mashed pumpkin
60 g (half cup) cake flour
5 ml (1 teaspoon) baking powder
A little salt
2 eggs, beaten
A little milk
Cinnamon-sugar

Mix the pumpkin, flour, baking powder and salt, and add egg and milk to make a soft batter. Heat fat or oil in a pan and ladle spoonsful of pumpkin mixture into it. Fry on both sides until brown, drain on paper and sprinkle with cinnamon-sugar.
Serve immediately with wedges of lemon.

Sweet potato fritters *(as dessert)*

500 ml (2 cups) sweet potato, cooked and mashed
60 g (half cup) cake flour
2 eggs, beaten
Cinnamon-sugar

Mix the sweet potato and flour and add egg and cinnamon-sugar to make a soft batter, adding a little milk if necessary. Form into patties and fry in hot fat. Serve with honey and lemon.

A later handwritten cookery book, the *Keuke boek* compiled by a widow named Blanckenberg, and bearing the date 1819, provides insight into the culinary art of the 1700s as well as the influence of English cookery at the turn of the 18th century. What makes this little book all the more interesting is that it consists of two parts; the first, in a neat flowing handwriting, contains numbered recipes from the VOC period, while the second part contains entries in English and reflects the English influence on Cape cookery after the British Occupation – an influence particularly noticeable in recipes for puddings and large cakes. Thus puddings of the Dutch period include traditional dishes such as milk, almond, lemon and rice tart, while plum pudding, Swiss roll, or simply 'pudding' are later additions. The development of baking techniques is also well illustrated: for example, in the first part mention is made only of those large cakes which were known before baking powders were introduced – cakes, such as sponge

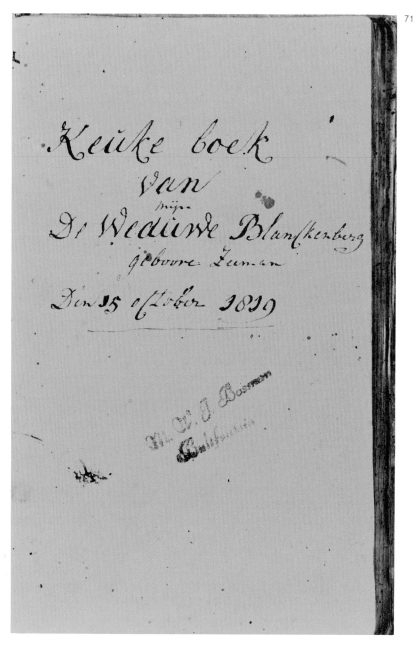

71 The title page of the widow Blanckenberg's cook book. **72** Pumpkin fritters done to a turn. Served with cinnamon-sugar and a squeeze of lemon juice, this is a typically South African dish though the suspended iron girdle-plate was probably brought to South Africa by Scottish settlers in about 1800.

7

cake, which were leavened with beaten egg whites, or with yeast (cakes referred to by the authoress as *dikkoek*). On the other hand, in the second part we come unexpectedly upon a 'Recipe of Mrs Thompson – Sal Volatile Cake' which is then followed by numerous recipes incorporating leavening agents such as sal volatile, cream of tartar and bicarbonate of soda.

The first cookery book printed in Afrikaans was *Kook- Koek- en Resepteboek* by E. J. Dijkman. She was born Elizabeth June Eckley in 1841 in London but emigrated as a young girl to the Cape where she later married a missionary by the name of Dijkman. She and her husband lived near Paarl and there she learnt Afrikaans and took a great interest in Afrikaans cookery. Over the years she collected and recorded the recipes of the wives of Cape farmers and these were published in 1890, when her husband was on the staff of the Paarlse Drukpers Maatskappy, in the language and spelling used by *Die Patriot,* the first Afrikaans newspaper.

74

Sosaties
Traditionally these are grilled over glowing hot coals. In the old days pickled sosaties were taken along as provisions (padkos) for a journey by ox-wagon or horse-drawn carriage. When the animals were unharnessed and allowed to rest at the outspan, the delicious aroma of braaivleis soon filled the air.

Cut approximately 1,5 kg leg of mutton into cubes. Sprinkle with salt and pepper and place in a deep dish rubbed with garlic. Cover with a mixture of sliced onion and lemon leaves and sprinkle with brown sugar. Pour half a cup (125 ml) milk over mixture.

The next day, make a marinade sauce by boiling together:

125 ml (half a cup) vinegar
60 g (8 level tablespoons) curry powder
12,5 ml (1 tablespoon) sugar
30 g (2 tablespoons) apricot jam
Salt

Allow to cool, add a few bayleaves and chopped chillies and cover the meat with the marinade sauce. Leave to stand for at least a day. Skewer alternate pieces of meat, fat and small onions on sharpened sticks or long slivers of Spanish reed. Grill the sosaties.

73 The *kakabeen wa* is outspanned, the *wakis* offloaded, the quilt spread on the turf and the hunting rifle is at rest. Sosaties and boerewors sizzle over the coals and the coffee kettle is on the hob. Dearest of all South African culinary traditions is the braaivleis and never more pleasurable than when it is enjoyed in the open veld. **74** Before the days of baking powder, bicarbonate of soda, cream of tartar and egg whites were used as raising agents as is seen from a page of the widow Blanckenberg's cook book.

Almond loaf *(served as cake)*

250 g mashed potatoes
250 g minced almonds
125 g sugar
5 eggs, separated
Pinch of salt

Mix all the ingredients except the eggs. Add the yolks to the other ingredients and mix. Whisk the egg-whites until stiff and fold in. Grease a flat bread pan with butter, sprinkle with breadcrumbs, pour in the batter, cover, and bake for an hour in a medium oven (180° C). Some of the old recipes recommend that almond loaf be served with citron preserves.

(A note to the old recipe indicates that 500 almonds weigh a pound. Almonds were often used in Cape cookery, usually with rose water to preserve the white colour.)

Raisin tart

Raw flaky pastry
150 g (1 cup) seedless raisins
250 ml (1 cup) water
80 g (third of a cup) sugar
25 ml (2 tablespoons) breadcrumbs
25 g (quarter cup) nuts
30 g (2 tablespoons) apricot jam
Pinch of salt
12,5 ml (1 tablespoon) cake flour
12,5 ml (1 tablespoon) lemon juice
5 ml (1 teaspoon) butter
1 egg-yolk
25 ml brandy (optional)

Bring raisins, sugar and water to the boil together. Add breadcrumbs, nuts, apricot jam and salt. Make a paste from the flour, lemon juice and a little water, and stir into the boiling raisin mixture. Add butter and allow to boil until thick and well cooked. Allow to cool slightly and then add the beaten egg-yolks and brandy. Spoon into a tart pan lined with raw flaky pastry and bake in a hot oven (200° C – 220° C) for 25 minutes.

Coconut tart

Flaky pastry
1 coconut or 120 g desiccated coconut
4 eggs
125 g (half cup) sugar

Grate the inside of the coconut very finely. Beat the eggs and sugar together, mix with the coconut and pour into a tart dish lined with flaky pastry. Bake in a hot oven (200° C) for 10 minutes, reduce temperature to 180° C and bake for another 10 minutes.

This small book which went through 18 editions, became a standard work on South African culinary history. An excerpt from the foreword reveals the need which the book filled at the time:

One of the most popular cookery books to appear when publications of this kind were still something of a novelty, was *Hilda's Where is it?* by Hildagonda Duckitt (published in 1891). Dr Anna de Villiers, an authority on the cultural history of the Cape, gives an informative evaluation of this work:

'Hildagonda Duckitt, whose mother was a Versfeld from the Darling area, likewise won fame for her cookery book *Hilda's Where is it?* This cookery book, however, differs considerably from the Dijkman cookery book on account of its ambiguous nature. Hilda arranged all the old recipes gathered from family members – among whom were members from quite prominent Cape families – alphabetically, but interspersed among them she added all kinds of other recipes for English, foreign and Eastern dishes that she had obtained from strangers or collected herself on her travels. She did indeed represent the typical tastes of the

75

well-to-do burghers at the Cape when she included items such as tomato bredie, curry, bobotie, bread dumplings, koeksisters, fritters, fricadels, fish kedgeree, yellow rice and pickled fish, Van der Hum liqueur, quince sambal, chutney, sour fig jam and abalone and even Malay dishes such as kebabs and sosaties. But

Black sour soup (*with dumplings*)
(*Hildagonda Duckitt's recipe*)

1,5 kg rib of mutton
1 onion
1 ℓ (approximately 4 cups) water
60 g tamarind seeds
2 eggs
6 cloves
Salt
12 peppercorns, crushed
7 ml (half tablespoon) brown sugar
120 g (1 cup) flour

Chop the mutton into pieces, add finely shredded onion and all the water and simmer for an hour to make a meat stock. Skim off one cup (250 ml) of stock and reserve the rest. To the cupful of stock, add the tamarind seed and other spices, salt and sugar, and allow to steep. To this add two cups (500 ml) of the reserve stock and boil to make the soup.

To make the dumplings, thicken one cup (250 ml) of meat stock with one cup (120 g) of flour and allow to cool. Stir two eggs into the mixture and form into dumplings the size of walnuts. Half an hour before serving, spoon the dumplings into the soup and steam. Serve at the beginning of a meal.

Black sour soup was originally made with pork, duck or chicken blood but tamarind seed was later substituted for blood in the recipe. This is the fruit of a tropical tree, Tamarindus indica, which looks and tastes like a sour plum.

75 The Cape housewife might have been a long way from Europe but this invaluable cookery book taught her the essentials of Dutch etiquette as well as how to cook. It was first published in 1761.

Sabanangvleis

500 g minced mutton
1 large onion
1 clove garlic
A knob of butter
500 g mashed potatoes
A little curry powder
A little milk
Cloves
A few bayleaves

Sauté finely chopped onion and garlic in butter.
Add meat and stir for 10 minutes while it is
braising. Mix meat and potatoes. Add curry
powder mixed with a little milk and blend.
Place in a shallow oven dish, garnish with
cloves, bayleaves and pats of butter and bake
for approximately half an hour in a medium
oven (180°C).

Meat curry

1,5 kg mutton
1 large onion
Butter and fat
250 ml (1 cup) tamarind water or 125 ml (half
cup) vinegar
10 ml (1 dessertspoon) sugar
12,5 ml (1 tablespoon) curry powder
Salt
Lemon leaves

Sauté the sliced onion in butter or fat. Cube the
meat, add to onion and simmer until the meat is
tender, adding water when necessary. Add the
rest of the ingredients and salt to taste. Serve
with rice and chutney.

Tamarynvleis

Prepare in the same way as meat curry but add
tamarind and a sprig of orange leaves with a
little yellow sugar instead of curry powder.

amongst all these you find Chicken Réchauffé, to mention but one.'

The cookery book *Cape Cookery, Simple yet Distinctive,* by Allie Hewitt, an English woman who lived in Sea Point, also dates from this period. Like Hildagonda Duckitt she, too, includes typical

South African recipes such as porcupine crackling, a dish which will not be found in other cookery books – but then there are also many foreign recipes such as mock *paté de foie gras*. Nevertheless, it is tastefully produced and the collection of recipes is divided into five categories: fish, meat, pastries, preserves and miscellaneous.

Another little book of this period does not fall into the category of traditional Afrikaans cookery: *The Colonial Household Guide by a Housewife of the Colony,* published in 1889. It was written by a Mrs A. R. Barnes, whose initials alone indicate her authorship, and was successful in its aim: to provide British women who had immigrated to South Africa with their own recipes such as 'bubble and squeak' and Yorkshire pudding, while at the same time introducing them to several dishes they would come across in their new home, dishes such as bean bredie and green spanspek konfyt.

These four printed cookery books were the only ones to appear in South Africa before 1900 and some of the original copies are treasured as priceless items by subsequent generations.

After the year 1900 a number of cookery books were published, but none was devoted specifically to traditional cookery. Popular books of the time included *Tafelvreugde,* which D. F. Malherbe of Bloemfontein had published in 1918; *Die Oranje Kook-, Koek- en Receptenboek voor Zuid-Afrika* of the same period, written by a 'Mrs D. J. H.' and adapted in 1931 by 'A Practical Housewife'

Fish soup with sherry

Mutton sabanang   Stewed sweet potatoes

Green beans in sour sauce

Guava salad

Rice dumplings with cinnamon-sugar

Coffee

Souskluitjies (cinnamon dumplings)
120 g (1 cup) cake flour
10 ml (2 teaspoons) baking powder
1 ml (quarter teaspoon) salt
12,5 ml (1 tablespoon) butter
1 egg
125 ml (half cup) milk
Cinnamon-sugar
Sift dry ingredients and rub in butter. Beat the egg and milk and mix in the dry ingredients to make a thick batter. Boil 500 ml water with a little salt in a large, shallow saucepan with a tight-fitting lid.
Spoon the batter into the boiling water with a teaspoon, each time dipping the spoon into the boiling water first. The dumplings must cook separately, not touching each other. Cover and simmer for about 10 minutes. Remove dumplings from water with perforated spoon, butter them lightly and spinkle with cinnamon-sugar. To make a sauce, stir cinnamon-sugar and butter into the water in which the dumplings were cooked.

Rice dumplings

500 ml (2 cups) cooked mashed rice
120 g (1 cup) cake flour
60 ml (quarter cup) boiling milk or water
4 well-beaten eggs
75 g (half cup) currants
12,5 ml (1 tablespoon) butter
12,5 ml (1 tablespoon) grated orange rind
Cinnamon-sugar
Mix all ingredients except the eggs together in a saucepan and heat. Allow to cool and add the eggs. Add more flour if batter is too thin. Then prepare in same way as cinnamon dumplings.

Peach pudding (or apricot pudding)
Grease a dish with butter and pour in a small glass (200 ml) of milk, followed by alternate layers of buttered bread cut into strips, and halved loose-stone peaches or apricots sprinkled with cinnamon-sugar. Pour a wine-glass of sweet wine over the full dish and bake in the oven. Serve with thin cream.

76 Dogs bark and bystanders stare as the farmer and his family arrive in Cape Town to sell their produce and buy their stores. **77** Porcupine was once considered a delicacy and Jan van Riebeeck declared that dassie meat was even more delicious than lamb. Old cookery books contain some strange recipes, including instructions for the preparation of these dishes – and also for scalloped tortoise!

Sponge cake was probably one of the first kinds of cake baked at the Cape. Many tin and copper sponge cake moulds – turban-shaped with a spout in the middle – have been preserved from the 18th century. At that time baking powder was not yet known but the air beaten into the eggs for sponge cake produced a light confection which seems to have been a general favourite.

It is interesting to note that some of the old sponge cake recipes gave the mass of the other ingredients in proportion to that of the eggs, and in those days, when people kept their own chickens, a dozen eggs might be used for one cake!

Sponge cake I

12 eggs (1 egg weighs approximately 60 g)
Sugar equal to the mass of the eggs (720 g)
Cake flour equal to the mass of 9 eggs (540 g)
10 drops petitgrain oil
12,5 ml (1 tablespoon) brandy

Beat the egg-yolks very briskly and stir in the sugar. Add well whisked egg-whites, followed by the flour, petitgrain oil and brandy. Stir the mixture lightly, pour into a well greased cake mould and bake immediately in a medium oven (180° C) until done.

Sponge cake II

6 eggs
Sugar equal to the mass of 5 eggs (300 g)
Cake flour equal to the mass of 3 eggs (180 g)
Juice of one lemon
1 ml (quarter teaspoon) salt

Place the sugar and flour in separate bowls in the oven and allow to become lukewarm. Separate the eggs and beat very well. As soon as the whites are stiff, add the beaten yolks and then the lemon juice. Fold in the sugar and then the flour. Bake in a well greased cake mould or pan in a medium oven (180° C) for one and a half to two hours. This sponge cake ought to be as light as a feather with a beautifully fine texture.

78 The generous scale of hospitality at the Cape was the settlers' heritage from their European forebears. Accustomed to kitchens of this size in their homelands, they were quite ready to prepare magnificent meals in their new country too.

under a new title *Lekkerkos;* and S. van Tulleken's *Praktiese Kookboek vir Suid-Afrika,* a comprehensive work published in 1922 in which the making of konfyt is especially well presented. This last book also reflects something of the new eating habits of the 20th century in the section entitled 'Lunch, Breakfast and Evening Dishes'.

The first cookery book written by a trained South African home economics graduate was *Mev. Slade se Afrikaanse Kookboek* which was published in 1923 by Jeanette van Duyn, a pioneer domestic science student who had studied in Canada and whose work as a result has a sound scientific basis but is subject to a strong American influence. Once home economics had become established as a field of study in South Africa, a number of graduates in the subject were employed by the then Department of Agriculture and, in 1933, the well-known *Kos en Kookkuns* was researched, compiled and published by home economists employed by the department. This standard work filled a great need and the first edition went out of print within four months. Subsequent revised editions containing new information have been published over the years and have kept the South African housewife up to date on cooking in a scientific way.

Although it lacked the scientific basis of the book mentioned above, the cookery book by the doctor-poet C. Louis Leipoldt was a rich source of information on herbs, spices and dishes for more sophisticated palates. Any lack his work may have in the scientific sphere is more than compensated for by Leipoldt's colourful descriptions. Of his earlier works, *Kos vir die Kenner* is the most important, and in 1976 an old manuscript of his was published under the title *Leipoldt's Cape Cookery.*

Other cookery books that deserve mention are the publications put out by food manufacturers such as the Royal Baking Powder Company whose *Anyone can Bake* was, after 1928, to be found in most South African homes, as well as Davis Gelatine's *Davis's Tasty Foods* which was distributed locally from 1922 onwards.

Today South African women have been able to enlarge their collections of recipe books and many of these later publications have been internationally acclaimed.

79 An ostrich egg omelette for breakfast, home-made potbread, fresh coffee near the old mill stream – a Little Karoo farmer would consider this the Cape culinary tradition at its best.

My sweetheart's in a tangerine
my grandmother in mace,
there's someone – yet who?
– in aniseed,
some half-remembered face.
*Translated from Sproeireën
by D. J. Opperman.*

'Aqua vitae, eau de vie, aqua ardens *or as we know it, brandy, was for many centuries the closely guarded secret of the apothecaries. This monopoly was ended by an historic event – the Spanish invasion of the Netherlands under the dreaded Duke of Alva. A group of highly skilled Dutch distillers escaped from the Spanish invaders and made their way to Brandenburg in northern Germany. There they used their skill to distil brandy from grape juice and sold it over the counter. It was during this time that brandy developed from an apothecary's distillate into a drink for the connoisseur.'* (From Prof. Mattie Jooste's description in Aqua Vitae.)

In the early days at the Cape, fruit was preserved in brandy and served in glasses as a dessert on special occasions.

Kaapsche Jongens *or* Korrelbrandewyn
(Brandied grapes)

Ripe Hanepoot grapes; brandy; castor sugar
Wash the ripe bunches well and snip off the grapes with stalks intact. Prick with a darning needle, pack into sterilised jars and sprinkle each layer with castor sugar. Fill the jars with brandy and screw tops closed. A fifty-fifty mixture of brandy and a heavy syrup made from equal amounts of sugar and water boiled together may be substituted for the brandy, but then the castor sugar should be omitted.

Boerejongens *(Brandied raisins)*

500 g washed raisins
Stick of cinnamon
250 g (1 cup) sugar
250 ml (1 cup) water
Boil all the ingredients for 10 minutes and then stir gently to make sure all the sugar is dissolved. Drain the raisins and pack them into sterilized jars. Fill the jars with brandy or with a mixture of the syrup and brandy in equal proportions.

Boeremeisies *(Brandied apricots)*

Ripe, firm, unblemished apricots
Brandy
Heavy syrup made from equal quantities of water and sugar boiled together.
Wash the apricots, prick with a darning needle and pack into sterilised jars. Mix brandy and syrup in equal quantities, fill the jars and replace screw-tops without tightening. Place a piece of wood or folded cloth in the bottom of a saucepan and stand the jars up to their necks in water in the saucepan. Heat to boiling point. Remove at once and seal.

80 Sunshine and the good earth give the ripe grapes their flavour; old oak and drowsing years add bouquet to the wine.

RECIPE INDEX

81 The fullness of the harvest. Beetroot, carrot, tomato and potato; matronly pumpkin and fresh young lettuce – all the fruits of the earth are here within the tranquil shadow of a white-washed South African gable.

BIBLIOGRAPHY

BARNARD, E. (1952): *Outydse Reseppies/Old-time Recipes*. Maskew Miller, Cape Town.

BAX, D. (1974): *Het Oudste Kaapse Zilver 1669-1751*. B. V. Noord-Hollandsche Uitgevers Maatschappij, Amsterdam.

BOËSEKEN, A. J. (1964): *Simon van der Stel en sy Kinders*. Nasou Ltd., Cape Town.

BOSMAN, D. B. (1952): *Briewe van Johanna Maria van Riebeeck en ander Riebeeckiana*. Drukkerij Holland N. V., Amsterdam.

BOTHA, C. G. (1962): *General History and Social Life of the Cape of Good Hope*. C. Struik, Cape Town.

COOK, MARY A. (1975): *The Cape Kitchen*. Stellenbosch Museum, Stellenbosch.

DE KOCK, V. (1955): *The fun they had: the pastimes of our forefathers*. Howard Timmins, Cape Town.

DE KOCK, V. (1963): *Those in Bondage*. Union Booksellers, Pretoria.

DE MIST, AUGUSTA (1954): *Diary of a Journey to the Cape of Good Hope and the Interior of Africa in 1802 and 1803*. A. A. Balkema, Cape Town.

DE VILLIERS, ANNA J. D. (1965): *Volksgebruike uit Vervloë Dae*. S.A.B.C., Johannesburg.

DE VILLIERS, ANNA J. D. (1966): *Ons Huisvlyt*. S.A.B.C., Johannesburg.

DUCKITT, H. J. (1891): *Hilda's 'Where is it?' of Recipes*. Chapman & Hall, London.

DU PLESSIS, I. D. (1947): *The Cape Malays*. Maskew Miller, Cape Town.

DIJKMAN, E. J. (1890): *De Suid Afrikaanse Kook-, Koek- en Resepte Boek*. Paarlse Drukpers, Paarl.

FORBES, W.A. (1969): *Antiek Bestek*. Van Dishoeck, Bussum, Holland.

FORBES, W. A. (1963): *De oudhollandse Keuken*. Van Dishoeck, Bussum, Holland.

FOUCHÉ, LEO (1970): *Dagboek van Adam Tas 1705 – 1706*. Van Riebeeck Society, Cape Town.

FRANKEN, J. L. M. (1938): *Duminy-dagboeke*. Van Riebeeck Society, Cape Town.

GERBER, HILDA (1959): *Traditional Cookery of the Cape Malays*. A. A. Balkema, Cape Town.

HEWITT, A. G. (1890): *Cape Cookery: Simple yet Distinctive*. Darter Bros & Walton, Cape Town.

HOPKINS, H. C. (1965): *Die Moeder van ons Almal. Geskiedenis van die Gemeente Kaapstad 1665-1965*. N.G. Kerk Publishers, Cape Town.

JOOSTE, MATTIE E. (1970): *Egte Suid-Afrikaanse Geregte* in Van der Merwe, C. P. and Albertyn, C. F. (Eds.). Die Vrou, Vol. II. C. F. Albertyn, Cape Town.

JOOSTE, MATTIE E. (1974): *Aqua Vitae*. Tydskrif vir Dieet- en Huishoudkunde Vol. 2, No. 1.

KINDERSLEY, MRS (1790): *Letters from Tenerife, Brazil, Cape of Good Hope and Indies*. J. Nourse, London.

KOLBE, PETER (1727): *Naaukeurige en Uitvoerige beschrijving van de Kaap de Goede Hoop*. B. Lakeman, Amsterdam.

LEIPOLDT, C. L. (1963): *Polfyntjies vir die Proe*. Tafelberg Publishers, Cape Town.

LICHTENSTEIN, H. (1928): *Travels in Southern Africa*. Van Riebeeck Society, Cape Town.

MENTZEL, O. F. (1925): *Description of the Cape*. Van Riebeeck Society, Cape Town.

MUILER-VAN BEUKSEKEN, C. A. H. (1972): *Culinaire Encyclopedie*. Elsevier, Amsterdam.

PARKER, MARY ANN (1795): *A Voyage around the World in the Gorgon Man of War*. John Nichols, London.

ROBINSON, A. M. L. (1973): *The letters of Lady Anne Barnard to Henry Dundas*. A. A. Balkema, Cape Town.

SCHOLTE-HOEK, C. H. A. (1965): *Het gastmaal en de tafel in de loop der tijden*. Elsevier, Amsterdam.

SCHOTEL, G. D. (1968): *Het Oud-Hollandsch Huisgezin der Zeventiende Eeuw*. A. C. Kruseman, Haarlem.

SHELL COMPANY (1940): *Voortrekkerresepte*. Shell South Africa Ltd.

SMITH, C. A.: *Common Names of South African Plants*. Government Printer, Pretoria.

SUID-AFRIKA Departement Nasionale Opvoeding, Seksie Huishoudkunde (1975): *Kos en Kookkuns*, Government Printer, Pretoria.

THOM, H. B. (1952): *Journal of Jan van Riebeeck*, Vol. I, II, III. Van Riebeeck Society, Cape Town.

TULLEKEN, S. VAN H. (1937): *Die Praktiese Kookboek vir Suid-Afrika*. Nasionale Pers Bpk., Bloemfontein.

VALENTYN, F. (1971): *Description of the Cape of Good Hope with the Matters concerning it*. Van Riebeeck Society, Cape Town.

VAN DEN HEEVER, C. M. AND PIENAAR, P. DE V. (1945): *Kultuurgeskiedenis van die Afrikaner*. Nasionale Pers Bpk., Cape Town.

VAN ESVELDT, S. (1965): *De Volmaakte Hollandse Keuken Meid*. A. W. Sijthoffs Uitgewersmaatschappij, Leiden.

VAN TONDER, I. W. (1950): *Van Riebeeck se Stad*. Juta & Co., Ltd., Cape Town.

VAN WINTER, J. M. (1971): *Van Soeter Cokene*. Grolsch, Bussum, Holland.

GENERAL INDEX

The numbers in italics refer to illustrations

Parker, Mary Ann 35, 80
Patriot, Die 109
pewter 72
pickles 45
pies 40
porcelain 77, 99
porcupine meat 26, *112*, 113
*Praktiese Kookboek vir
  Suid-Afrika* 116
preserves (see jam)
Prionum palmita 50
Protea arborea 20
Protea repens 53
pumpkin fritters 106, *107*

Renier, François 46
Rhus lucida 50, 53
Ribes grossularia 23
rice, cultivation 25
Ricinodendron rautanenii 49
rissoles *30-31*
Romulea longifolia 53
Rubus fructicosus 23

salad 50
Saldanhers (Saldaniers) 25
sambal 45
sauces 43
sausage 44, *64*, 65, 66-67
Saxifragaceae 23
Scorzonera hispana 22
seaweed jelly 79, *87*

shellfish 47
silverware 77, 78
silversmiths 53, 78
soetkoekies 40, 78
sosaties 46, 109
spices 18, 28, 40, 43, 45, 67-68, 99
stampkarring 21
Stellenbosch 34, 38, 92
Strandlopers 17, 25, 48
sugarbush 55
Swartland 38
Swellendam 38
Swellengrebel, Governor 70

taaibos 53
table linen 72, 79
tafelvreugde 113
Tas, Adam 34, 68, 80, 89
tea 24, 80
tempies 61
tessie *51*, 81
toekos 69, 70
trek boers 38, 47-48, 68
Tulbagh (town) 38, 103
Tulbagh, Ryk 70, 102

uintjie 56

Valentyn, François 21, 35, 94
Van der Hum, Admiral 55
Van der Stel, Simon 34, 35, 37, *40*,
  78, 92, 94

Van der Stel, Willem Adriaan 38,
  94, 99
Van Duyn, Jeanette 116
Van Passel, Jan 24
Van Plettenberg, Governor 38
Van Riebeeck, Abraham 23, 24
Van Riebeeck, Jan 17, 18, 21-28,
  33, 34, 50, 57, 58, 61, 65, 72, 88,
  94, 102, 105
Van Riebeeck, Johanna 18, 34, 105
Van Riebeeck's Journal 21, 24, 28,
  33
Van Tulleken, S. 116
vegetables 21, 35, 39, 49
Vereenigde Oost-Indische
  Compagnie 17, 22, 36, 37
– monogram 77, 78
Vergelegen 94
viticulture (see under 'wine')
*Volmaakte Hollandse Keukenmeid,
  De* 50, *110*
Von Dessin, Joachim 70, 89

waffles 40
Wagenaar, Zacharias 33
wateruintjies (waterblommetjies) 49,
  49, 56
Waveren, Land of the 38
Wild Almond (see under *Brabeium
  stellatifolium*)
wine 23, 34, 38, 44, 80-81